# Praise for Reggie Marra's Work

*Killing America* (Poetry, 2018)

"Reggie Marra's poetry is both raw and sobering, highlighting how violence changes everything it 'touches' either by design or by default, whether we are participants or spectators.... The spectrum of violence can't be eliminated; it can be minimized if understood. This book helps us do that."

  *- Bob Killackey,* Marine Infantry Officer, Combat Veteran, Husband, Parent, and Public High School Teacher

"Reggie Marra's searing, soul-screaming poetry addresses the wielding of power within a democracy....while shining an unbearable light on the victims of a million American bullets, of children dead, communities ravaged..."

  *- Joan Hurley,* Mother, 2008 Connecticut Teacher of the Year

*And Now, Still* (Poetry, 2016)

"Openhearted, rich in detail, and wildly irreverent, Reggie Marra's *And Now, Still* celebrates the sacred everyday connections among the living, the dying, and the dead.... A generous collection that defies being boxed, this book is a healing journey offered by a kind, resilient, skillful and eloquent guide."

  *- Janet E. Aalfs,* author, *Bird of a Thousand Eyes,* founder & director of *Lotus Peace Arts,* http://www.vwma.org/

"Reggie Marra's poetry speaks to me deeply of hope and joy, beautifully woven into the context of grief and loss.... Reggie has the ability to gather precious moments and offer them as a gift to the reader. I recommend slowly sipping and savoring each word that it may touch and magnify your life."

  *- Joanna Burgess-Stocks,* BSN, RN, CWOCN, Patient Advocate

## *The Quality of Effort* (Nonfiction, 2013, 1991)

"*The Quality of Effort* inspires coaches and parents to divert their eyes from the scoreboard and focus on nurturing the heart, mind and body of today's young athlete. Reggie Marra offers a blueprint that encourages our children to become not only better athletes but better people...."

  - *Anthony Perrone,* VP, Challenger Division, Cortland American Little League

Reggie Marra has, with a master's touch and rapier wit, illustrated that the essential value of effort is in the quality of the lesson we have learned—and not in the victory or defeat on the field of battle. The book is an incredibly personal gift from Reggie to the reader, written through and with his bountiful, open heart."

  - *Tom Rubens,* Founder, The Accountability Factor

"*The Quality of Effort* has helped me reinterpret my career as a professional athlete – providing both relief and direction....Reggie Marra offers a map to tomorrow's competitive edge, a map that requires effort – not necessarily in doing more drills or pushups, but in taking responsibility for all aspects of your approach to life."

  - *Ryan Leech,* Professional Mountain Biker (Retired) and Professional Integral Coach™

"After reading this book, I wish I could redo my entire childhood sports experience....While I credit baseball with saving my life by keeping me off the street and away from the wrong crowd, I never gave much thought to how much it has made me a better husband, father, friend, and business owner. After reading *The Quality of Effort,* I get it."

  - *Robert Gambardella,* CPA, CTA, owner, Concierge Tax Services

"As a former college athlete and longtime leader of high-performance military units, I recommend Reggie Marra's work with unbridled enthusiasm.... How much happier we would all be if we could travel a healthy path of development supported by quality practices, competent and caring coaches/teachers, and a nurturing learning environment."

  - *Fred Krawchuk,* Retired U.S. Special Forces Colonel, Strategist, Social Innovator, Peacemaker

*Coaching and Healing: Transcending the Illness Narrative*
    (Nonfiction, 2016, co-authored with Joel Kreisberg, Jon Stoddart, Lois MacNaughton, Leslie Williams, Amy Phillips, Karin Hempel, Julie Flaherty, Alex Douds & Jill Lang Ward)

"I highly recommend this book as a healing narrative and an illustration of what can be accomplished when human beings put their minds together for healing purposes."
    - *Lewis Mehl-Madrona*, MD, PhD, author, *Coyote Medicine* and *Narrative Medicine*

"It is perhaps no accident that Reggie Marra is a poet as well as a healing coach. The moving narratives he and his colleagues have chosen for this book reflect a poet's thinking, that is, a creative vision of what healing is beyond the rigid medical conventions."
    - *Doug Anderson*, author, *Horse Medicine*, and *Keep Your Head Down: A Memoir – Vietnam, the Sixties, and a Journey of Self-Discovery*

"In *Coaching and Healing*, Dr. Joel Kreisberg and his colleagues describe a new model of patient care…based on an integral perspective – attention not just to the physcial aspects of a client, but also his or her psychological, social and spiritual needs….This approach should be part of the skill set of anyone involved in patient care."
    - Larry Dossey, MD, author, *One Mind,* and *Reinventing Medicine*

"In this powerfully rendered, honest, and deeply wise book, the authors guide coaches in establishing the kind of coaching relationships that transcend the fixation on cures, and serve the deepest domain of healing and realizing inner freedom."
    - Tara Brach, PhD, author, *Radical Acceptance* and *True Refuge*

"Whether you are in the midst of your own healing journey or providing care to someone who is, *Coaching and Healing* will give you fresh and powerful ways to understand healing at a deep level."
    - Laura Divine and Joanne Hunt, Co-Founders, Integral Coaching Canada, Inc.

"...*Coaching and Healing* pioneers a new area of research and pratice, namely, the application of Integral Coaching to the process of healing.... [and] demonstrates the clear importance and profound effectiveness of taking a more integral approach to the whole process of illness and healing."

- Ken Wilber, author, *Integral Meditation* and *Integral Spirituality*

## *This Open Eye: Seeing What We Do* (Poetry, 2006)

"Reggie Marra writes with stunning, graphic precision—brutal scenes the American news skips over, scenes of endless sorrow that politicians bury under false phrases like 'total victory'....These poems are tributes to the nearly-invisible wounded and the honest humanity so many of us yearn for now."

- Naomi Shihab Nye, author, *Cast Away, Voices in the Air, Transfer, You & Yours;* National Book Award Finalist, *19 Varieties of Gazelle*

"*This Open Eye* is a powerful, devastating, and stunningly beautiful book. Reggie Marra has unfalteringly absorbed the images and voices of the war in Iraq, pared them down to the bone, and handed them back to us that we, too, might bear witness to our times. Not in any of these poems, or the essay, has he taken the easy way out. Like Breyten Breytenbach, Nelly Sachs, and Antonio Machado before him, Marra reclaims the essentially human from both the brutal and the brutalized."

- *Trebbe Johnson*, author, *Radical Joy for Hard* Times and *The World is a Waiting Lover: Desire and the Quest for the Beloved.*

# Enough
*with the...*

Unconscious • Partial • Habitual • Ignorant
Disingenuous • Manipulative • Literal
Radical • Metaphorical • Irrelevant
Conservative • Libertarian • Republican
Female • Democrat • Male • Liberal
Capitalist • Sexist • Reactionary • Socialist
Racist • Otherwise Bigoted • Eye-rolling
Head-shaking • Smirking • Snide
*(pick one or more and/or add your own)*

# Talking Points

*Doing More Good than Harm
in Conversation*

## REGGIE MARRA

From the Heart Press
*2020*

Copyright © 2019, 2020 by Reggie Marra
All Rights Reserved
Manufactured in the United States of America

Published by From the Heart Press
More information at: https://reggiemarra.com/

*Enough with the...Talking Points:*
*Doing More Good than Harm in Conversation*
ISBN: 978-0-9627828-9-3
Library of Congress Control Number: 2020907678

First Printing: June 2020

Author Photograph: Tracy Burke
Cover Design: Reggie Marra

For everyone who intentionally speaks and acts in increasingly authentic, inclusive, comprehensive, balanced, compassionate, wise and vulnerable ways – aware of, honoring and embracing our common origin, planet, life and humanity.

~

And in grateful memory of John Prine (1946-2020) who joyfully shared with us the difference between a half an inch of water and a happy enchilada, the mixed blessings of a cigarette that's nine miles long, and other essential truths in this big old goofy world.
We're glad you liked the words, John.

Also by Reggie Marra

POETRY

*Killing America: Our United States of Ignorance, Fear, Bigotry, Violence and Greed* (2018)

*And Now, Still: Grave & Goofy Poems* (2016)

*This Open Eye: Seeing What We Do* (2006)

*Who Lives Better Than We Do?* (2001)

PROSE

*Coaching and Healing: Transcending the Illness Narrative* (2016)
with Joel Kreisberg, Jon Stoddart, Lois MacNaughton,
Leslie Williams, Amy Phillips, Karin Hempel,
Julie Flaherty, Alex Douds & Jill Lang Ward

*Integral Coaching and Healing* (2016)
with Robert Wright, Jr. and Christine Wright

*Grief and Healing* (2016)
with Robert Wright, Jr. and Christine Wright

*The Quality of Effort* 2nd Edition (2013)

*The Quality of Effort Workbook* (2013)

*Living Poems, Writing Lives: Spirit, Self and the Art of Poetry* (2004)

*The Quality of Effort: Integrity in Sport and Life for Student-Athletes, Parents and Coaches* (1991)

# CONTENTS

Introduction     i

### *Part One*
*Knowing Yourself, Your Biases and Your View –
Working with What and How You See*

1. Who (You Think) You Are in Conversation:
   Part 1 – The Culture Thing     3

2. Who (You Think) You Are in Conversation:
   Part 2 – Within and Beyond Culture     13

3. Recognizing and Suspending Preconceptions,
   Judgments and Assumptions     21

### *Part Two*
*Honoring Facts and Identifying Opinions – Really?
Will That Hold Up in Court or in the Laboratory?*

4. Avoiding Labels, Insults and Sweeping
   Generalizations     27

5. Getting Clear on and Honoring the Difference
   Between Opinion and Fact     31

6. Antidotes for Generalizations, Labels and
   Insults: Get Specific, Factual, Personal &
   Aware of Others     37

### Part Three
*Learning Intentionally – How Do You Want to Be, and What Do You Hope for, in this Conversation?*

7. Curiosity, Knowing and Not Knowing on the Path of Learning — 47

8. Conversing in Order to Learn, Understand and Gain Clarity, Rather than Trying to Teach, Persuade or Disprove — 53

### Part Four
*Acknowledging the Forest and Staying on the Path – Wow, You're Human Too!*

9. Finding Similarities as Well as Differences in Disagreement — 59

10. Committing to and Actually Staying Focused on the Topic of the Current Conversation — 65

### Part Five
*Emotion, Empathy and Ripple Effects – Feeling, Honoring and Regulating Emotions*

11. Listening for and Feeling into the Emotions that Lead to and Emerge from Your Own and Others' Words and Actions — 73

12. Understanding, Feeling, Embodying and Telling Another's Story as if It Were Your Own — 79

13. What's the Impact of (Not) Getting My Way: What Will Be Won and Lost and by Whom? — 83

## *Part Six*
### *Understanding "Truth" and "Truthfulness"*

14. The Truth, the Whole Truth and Nothing
    but the Truth     91

15. Stepping Back and Moving Forward: Bringing
    a Bigger Picture into View     97

Selected Resources     101

# Introduction

The title of the series of sixteen blogs from which this book emerged was *Guidelines for Adult Conversation.* Perhaps clever (or not) when the blogs appeared from January through May, 2019, that title required an increasingly clear definition of "adult," which, over time, proved problematic at best. Other prospective, serious and less serious titles for the blog and this book include:

- Disagreeing (and Agreeing) With Civility
- Blah, Blah, Blah: Just Another Talking Point
- Silence May Have Been Better
- Who (Do You Think) You Are, and What (in the World) Do You Mean by *That?*
- I'm Right and You're Wrong
- You Can't Be Serious
- Why Don't You Shut Up?

The intention of this writing is for all of us who speak or write to become increasingly better able to deeply listen to others, and authentically express ourselves, in ways that foster understanding, appreciation and respect for everyone who is present, and everyone who is not. With some few exceptions, "we" seem to have lost the ability to disagree with each other without engaging in personal insult, labeling and sweeping generalizations. We also seem to have lost the ability to *agree* with each other without engaging in personal insult, labeling and sweeping generalizations directed toward those who are *not* present, with whom we disagree.

This loss of ability (or lack of skill, or chosen laziness, or (in)-vincible ignorance...) is evident with just about anyone who wishes the world were different, who *knows* who's to blame for how the world is, and who's sure that he or she is not part of the problem, but rather a victim, a prospective savior, or both. It is tempting to begin listing specific groups (elected officials, news commentators, pharmaceutical executives, billionaires, etc.) after "...is evident with..." above, but the list would be too long, inevitably incomplete, and in some ways contrary to this book's intention. So, whether you believe that Conservative-Republican-Capitalist-Homophobic-Fascists, Liberal-Democrat-Socialist-LGBTQ-Bleeding Hearts, Independent Infidels or some combination of these is to blame for everything that's wrong, YOU *are* part of the problem. That sentence is an example of what this book argues against saying or writing. If you're interested in engaging what the book argues *for,* I invite you to keep reading.

Chapters One and Two explore the essential task of knowing ourselves, with Chapter One's focus on the often invisible hand of culture and collective worldview, which is complemented by Chapter Two's focus on the often just as invisible hand of individual genetics, direct experience (especially, but not only in childhood), personality, health, work, finance, friendship and other factors that further impact how each of us sees and experiences life. More simply, each of us sees through a worldview that is influenced and formed by both the larger cultural and our smaller individual characteristics. To the extent we are aware of this, we can be increasingly conscious and intentional with our thoughts, emotions, words and behaviors. To the extent we are unaware of these multiple influencers, they can, quite literally, run our lives. It comes down to whether we are aware that we have these influencers in our lives, or, unaware of them, they have us.

To the point of this book, it's essential to get to know ourselves and our worldviews – our values, beliefs and biases, and the experiences and other learnings that inform them, and to commit to this learning and knowing as an ongoing, lifelong process – especially, but not only, if we want to engage in meaningful conversation with others.

Directly related to our awareness of worldview or lack thereof, Chapter Three explores our ability to recognize and suspend our preconceptions, judgments and assumptions in order to better differentiate what is truly ours and what belongs to the other(s) in conversation.

Chapter Four zeroes in on that example of what not to do (above, page ii, first full paragraph) and provides both the *why* and some of the *how* we need in order to avoid insults, labels and sweeping generalizations in both our disagreements and our agreements.

In Chapter Five we'll work on getting clear on and honoring the difference between opinion and fact, where fact refers to an event or characteristic that reasonable, competent individuals, regardless of their beliefs or opinions, agree on, and opinion refers to the meaning(s) an individual ascribes to a fact or another opinion. *This room is too cold!* is an opinion. *The thermometer reads 68 degrees* is a fact (even if the thermometer is broken). And yes, it's often more complicated than that.

Chapter Six follows and deepens the preceding two chapters' explorations of insults, labels, generalizations, facts and opinions and makes the argument for providing specific, factual and whenever possible, personal examples to support our opinions – as opposed to characterizing, generalizing and interpreting the opinions of others.

Chapter Seven revisits the first two chapters' work with worldview and explores the rationale for and possible ramifications of getting and staying genuinely curious about ourselves, others and the world – and engaging and embracing the at-times paradoxical gift of 'not knowing' as we learn in our attempts to 'know'.

Chapter Eight explores conversational intention – what it is we intend in conversation with others, and recommends listening and speaking in order to learn, understand and clarify, rather than to teach, persuade or discredit (unless teaching or persuasion has been agreed upon by participating parties in, or is the explicit purpose of, the conversation). For example: in the "expert model" in medicine, in which doctors have knowledge and expertise, they explore and address patients' symptoms, and try to cure them – curing is the explicit intention. A different intention invites doctors to actually listen to their patients and their stories and see them as fully human beings, rather than symptom carriers that need to be fixed – not to ignore or minimize the doctors' expertise, but to orient the conversation in a different way – toward ongoing, intentional, integrated health and wellbeing, rather than waiting and then fixing what is perceived as broken.

Chapter Nine invites us to commit to finding those places where we actually agree with the other, and not just where we disagree. Seeking and acknowledging similarities as well as differences can be a remarkably simple step toward healing in a difficult conversation.

In Chapter Ten we're asked to agree to, and actually stay focused on, the specific content of the current conversation. Creating conversational boundaries allows us to avoid the traditional political debate perversion: a moderator asks a specific question (which is often a 'gotcha' aimed at one or more candidates), and the candidates ignore the question and spew forth their prepared talking points about whatever they want. Success with this work relies heavily on the conversational parties' *intention* (Chapter Eight). We are more likely to agree to and stay focused on a particular topic if our intention is to understand, learn and clarify.

Chapter Eleven invites us to feel into and listen for the emotion(s) behind our own and others' words. Much has been written and said about the importance of "emotional intelligence" since the 1990's. The abilities to recognize, differentiate, name and regulate our emotions, as with our stories, assumptions and biases, allows us to have emotions rather than being had by them – a crucial skill amid a disagreement.

While the work in chapters one through eleven is not particularly easy to engage, Chapter Twelve asks us to significantly up our game by learning *to understand, feel, embody and tell the other's story as if it were our own,* which challenges us to move beyond the idea of walking in another's shoes – which is a good place to start and useful, and which has limitations that we'll explore.

Chapter Thirteen, in the spirit of the late Neal Postman and others, asks us to honestly explore and assess how what we promote and what we protest impacts others, especially others who are "not like us" – in the broadest meaning of those last three words. Put differently, "Who stands to lose, and how and what will they lose, and who stands to win, and how and what will they win, if what we promote truly manifests and what we protest truly disappears?"

Chapter Fourteen complements Chapter Five's differentiation of fact and opinion, and engages our navigation of "the truth," all of it, with no additional additives, or as the traditional oath puts it, to tell *the truth, the whole truth, and nothing but the truth.*

Chapter Fifteen steps back and reflects on what has preceded it in an attempt to honestly assess what might be both relevant and beyond the scope of this book.

Finally, as the final draft of this book was coming into view in early 2020, the COVID-19 pandemic was beginning to make itself known on the planet. As I type this sentence this morning here in Connecticut, about 90 miles from New York City, the death toll on the planet is over 300,000 and the number of confirmed cases is approaching 5 million. Those statistics will be different and higher, unfortunately, by the time you hold this book in your hands.

The pandemic is bringing out both the best and the worst of our species at the same time it confirms, validates and reminds us that we really do share this planet and rely on each other in many ways. We get to see in real time the diversity of responses to both the virus and the attempts to contain and treat it – responses that are grounded in diverse levels of awareness that include "it's about *me,*" "it's about *us,*" – to whomever "us" might refer; "it's about *all of us,*" and "it's about *all that is*" – each of which has a unique impact on those who see that way, and on how they see others.

It's not too late to learn how to listen to and speak with each other.

# Part One

*Knowing Yourself, Your Biases and Your View – Working with What and How You See*

# 1.

# Who (You Think) You Are in Conversation: Part 1 – the Culture Thing

What do *you* bring into conversation? What is it that informs the stances you take, the opinions you hold, the beliefs you defend? How aware are you of these stances, opinions and beliefs, and what's behind them?

To help clarify your responses to the above inquiries (and to begin in a not-so-subtle way), briefly, or at length, consider these four issues. What's your honest response to each? 'Simply' see and feel what comes up for you around each of these:

- To what extent should government or religion be involved in a woman's choosing whether to have an abortion?
- What causes the unprecedented number of mass shootings and other gun violence in the United States?
- Why should or shouldn't the United States provide reparation to the descendants of slaves?
- What led to the September 11, 2001 attacks?[1] More on this one below.

This chapter explores some components that each of us brings to conversation – and to everything else we do: beliefs, values, experiences and points of view that make us who we (think we) are. This self-knowing, and paradoxically the 'not knowing' that accompanies it, is essential in conversation if any one of us wants to be clear on "what's mine," "what's yours" and "what's ours" when we speak.

In "The Inner Experience" Thomas Merton invites us to consider that any time we utter a first-person pronoun regarding our opinions, values, hopes or fears, we should first check to see if there is really some discrete human being behind it. When any one of us speaks about *my* beliefs, values and opinions, it is incumbent upon him or her to make sure there truly is an *I* who is speaking and not "the anonymous authority of the collectivity speaking through [my] mask."[2] The influence of this collective, anonymous authority cannot be overstated.

Some forty years after Merton penned those words, in *Integral Spirituality,* Ken Wilber, writing about the power of collective developmental structures and viewpoints, describes an individual as having "no idea that he is the mouthpiece of this structure....", and that it is "the structure itself that is speaking through him..."[3] The underlying themes of traditional, modern and postmodern values structures – among others, and the transitions between them, can be quite readily recognized by a competent reader or listener.

Both Merton and Wilber point to the often invisible impact of culture on our individual viewpoints; Wilber's assessment adds a developmental component that was not available as such in Merton's time; and culture *is just one* of the forces, albeit it a powerful one, that influences how each of us shows up in the world. Was that me, or was it the tenets of Christianity, Islam, capitalism, socialism, modernity or some other collective view speaking through me? Good question.[4]

As used here, the word *culture* refers to the underlying, often 'invisible' unless, and often even *if,* intentionally explored, systems of beliefs, values and perspectives that influence, inform and even create our views – effectively the 'givens' into which any one of us is born – at a specific time, in a specific place. Typically, such culture is comprised of various subcultures. An example follows; as you read it, reflect on the parallel characteristics of the 'givens' in your own life – whether or not you have embraced, adapted or rejected them:

> I was born on May 28, 1954 in Yonkers NY in the United States. Both my parents were first-generation Italian-American Catholics, whose parents came through Ellis Island between 1895 and 1906. My mom was 38 and my dad was 47 when I was born. Married in 1952 at 36 and 45 respectively, they brought my sister into the world almost 9 months to the day after their wedding; I followed 11 months later. A first-grade teacher, my mom was first in her family to attend and graduate college (CUNY - Hunter College). My dad graduated high school, served in the Pacific in the Navy during World War II, made his living as a plumber, and as did many men of his generation, spoke of having attended the 'college of hard knocks'.
>
> My parents' 9 siblings combined to give me 34 cousins in 9 families spread across Yonkers, the lower Hudson Valley, Staten Island and Long Island – many of whom we saw with some regularity on weekends and holidays.
>
> I grew up in suburban Yonkers with lots of chronological peers and several close friends on my block and on surrounding streets, with sports fields adjacent to the elementary schools mentioned below, and ample wooded areas near and along the Saw Mill River. Most of the houses were built eight-to-an-acre on 50' x 100' plots.
>
> I attended public school from kindergarten through 2$^{nd}$ grade, including religious instruction at the local parish once a week, then transferred across the street to the newly built Catholic school for grades 3 through 8. Both schools were a 10-minute walk from home, so I could eat lunch at home. I attended a co-ed Catholic high school about 3 miles away, and eventually, received a bachelor's

degree from St. John's University in Jamaica, NY, and a master's from Iona College in New Rochelle.

Beyond the above basics, my early years included doctors who still made house calls; black and white television with 7 stations available, with signals received through a roof antenna and/or 'rabbit ears' atop the TV; early childhood New York biases handed down from my dad, uncles and cousins toward the Yankees & football Giants; later childhood and adolescent biases from a cousin and a local older neighbor, toward basketball; self-discovered competence, along with my best friend, in middle-long distance running; and the blessing of learning that when I did my work and studied, I performed well academically.

Obviously, there is a lot more detailed information both within and beyond the categories I've selected to share. I'll choose several larger social perspectives to build on to make the point:

The national, regional, state, local, religious, educational, media and familial cultures into which I was born and in which I was raised early on 'gave' my childhood self a (world)view that conveyed various "truths" that included:

- I lived in the greatest country in the world because it was a democracy and won the wars it fought.
- Other democracies were not as great as my country because they relied on us, especially in war.
- Japan and Germany were bad countries and we were giving them a chance to redeem themselves after World War II – various people, books, movies and television shows made this clear.
- Cowboys were good guys, Indians were savages, but there were some good Indians like Tonto; again movies and television backed this up.
- Slavery was a bad thing, but Abraham Lincoln and the Civil War ended it.

- Catholicism was the one true religion, and we had a relationship with the Jews through something called the Judeo-Christian tradition. We called their writings the Old Testament, and the story of Jesus's life the New Testament. Jewish people messed up by not accepting Jesus as the Savior that God had promised them.
- According to the Baltimore Catechism, God was *the Supreme Being who made all things;* Jesus was his only Son, and together with a magical, mystical bird known as the Holy Ghost or Holy Spirit, they formed the Holy Trinity.
- If I said certain prayers a specified number of times, I could limit the time I might spend in purgatory, where I'd go if I didn't get to heaven right away, but was good enough not to go to hell.
- I was expected, as a child, to defer to all authority, which meant pretty much any adult. Many of my friends' parents were referred to as "aunt" and "uncle" and all of them kept an eye on all of us when we were young.
- The Yankees were the greatest baseball team in history; no other team came close in terms of World Series championships (okay, this one actually holds up ☺).

Upon reflection, the worldview I was given as a child was a blend of what I might today call mythic and rational. While science was an important subject in school, certain "non-scientific" "mythic truths" were *given* and it was my job to embrace and honor these "truths" about God and country as they were handed down to me. To do otherwise would be to lose my faith or be unpatriotic, either of which would carry unpleasant consequences. Being faithful and patriotic in the greatest country ever and worshipping according to the one true Church were safe ways to be a kid. They were also limited, limiting and even *wrong* – in terms of both what was known and not taught or shared, and what was not yet known, available to, or accessible by the majority of the culture at the time.

What's above is an incomplete summary of what I was given at birth and during childhood, and here's its obvious, and easy to forget importance: *every person born anywhere and at any time since humans first appeared has his or her own set of givens* – in every location (whether or not nations were formed yet), with or without religion (for those who were born after religions were formed), and in poverty and wealth (however those two concepts might have been experienced at the time and place of each birth). You get the idea, yes? Each of us has a *given* story – an initial set of givens – whether or not we are aware of it. Some of it is given in order to simplify a complex world for young children; some of it is given as literal truth by the adults who believe it.

Each of us continues to be 'given' more through late childhood, adolescent, young adult, and adult experience and observation.[5] My childhood and adolescence included, among much else, the assassinations of John F. Kennedy, Malcolm X, Martin Luther King, Jr. and Robert F. Kennedy; the war in Vietnam; Woodstock; the Cold War with the USSR; and the moon landing. More personally and locally, I often went to work with my father on weekends when he was called for plumbing 'emergencies' – and I learned some cool lessons about him, his trade and people in general; I got to experience the 1969-1970 New York Knicks NBA Championship (while getting cut from my high school and university basketball teams) and was deeply moved, at the age of 16 by the emerging story of Kris Kristofferson's life as a college athlete, Golden Gloves boxer, award-winning fiction writer, Rhodes Scholar, US Army Ranger Captain and helicopter pilot, singer-songwriter and movie star – all by his mid-thirties – a trajectory that *my* givens would never have thought possible.

An oversimplified, but not without merit way of looking at the impact of these early givens and how we live our lives suggests that we may embrace and/or rebel against some or all of what our culture-of-origin gives (imposes upon) us. The *and/or* component is, itself, oversimplified. More granularly, we engage one or more of the following moves, sometimes intentionally and sometimes unintentionally. Whenever life events either reinforce or undermine our early givens, we may:

- embrace all that we were given
- reject all that we were given
- embrace some and reject some of what we were given
- embrace early on, and reject some as we grow older
- reject early on, and sometime later, re-embrace the original or an adapted version of it

*How* we hold these embraces, rejections and adaptations is intimately connected with the specifics of *what* we have actually embraced, rejected or adapted (that may warrant a second reading). When a member of a religious family stops practicing the public rituals (e.g. going to Mass on Sundays for Catholics), some members of the family and the larger religious community may begin speaking about a "loss of faith," based in a belief that such cessation of public practice is a 'straying' from the path or falling away from God. Other members of the family and the larger community may see this cessation as anything from simple laziness to a courageous and necessary finding one's own way in the world – or said differently, a natural part of development. What we're concerned with in this specific example is the extent to which each of us, in conversation, is aware of where we stand along this "loss of faith" / "finding one's own way" continuum – and along many other worldview continua that impact what and how we see.

This chapter is beginning an exploration of *you,* so that in conversation you know increasingly more clearly, who and how you are. What informed your earliest years, how aware of it are you, and what informs you today?

Let's return now to those four questions at the beginning of the chapter, and take a closer look at the fourth – regarding what led to the September 11, 2001 attacks. Again, we're not concerned here with *what* your response might be – we're interested in what you can learn about yourself based on *how* you respond. Some of the early 'explanations' offered in response to what happened that day in New York City, Washington, D.C. and Pennsylvania include:

- The hijackers were jealous of the freedoms, wealth and abundance enjoyed in the United States. As they saw more and more of the manifestations of these freedoms, wealth and abundance via various media, they attempted to destroy what they could not have themselves.

- God was punishing New York City for its sins – especially homosexuality and the greed inherent in the corporate cultures of Wall Street, Madison Avenue and Fifth Avenue.

- Islam is a violent religion whose followers are unable or unwilling to adjust to the modern world, have no respect for women and consider non-Muslims to be infidels who must be converted or killed.

- Some Saudis, represented by 15 of the 19 hijackers, were angry over their king's welcoming tens of thousands of U.S. troops, rather than raising their own forces (as they had helped Afghanistan do against the Soviet Union) ostensibly to help prevent an attack by Iraq after that country had invaded Kuwait.

- Israel had masterminded the attack in order to solidify U.S. support against Arab enemies (another version claims the C.I.A conspired with Israel on this), especially since there were increasingly more hints of support in the United States for Palestinians.

- Thousands of civilians had been killed in U.S. military action in the Middle East since 1980, and a group of men figured out a way to fight back against the superior power of the United States, much as colonists had done against Great Britain in the 1770's.

These will suffice. Keep your focus on exploring your worldview, and perhaps, where it comes from. We're not making a case for any of the above scenarios.

## Who (You Think) You Are

Three ways you can work with this right now:

1. Spend some time inquiring into what beliefs, values, and experiences might lead someone to hold any one or more of the above responses. *Really inquire*; don't just guess, or mock those statements with which you disagree.

2. Reread each of the above bullet points and pay close attention to how your belly, your heart and your mind react to each. What is it about you and your worldview such that you react as you do?

3. Do some research into which, and to what extent any, of the responses are backed up by empirical evidence (i.e. facts – which we'll explore in more detail in Chapters 5 and 14). You can conduct a similar experiment with any issue, large, small, personal, professional, political, etc. It's not about the issue. It's about you, your views and how you hold them (so, there).

4. Beyond the specific inquiry above, begin writing *your* "cultural givens" summary. Use my example on pages 5-7 as a model of one way to go about it. Take your time and allow it to unfold. See how influential it is in your life today.

~

In Chapter Two, we'll explore several other components that influence who each of us (thinks he or she) is. Our goal is to begin to recognize the lenses through which we see and experience the world in order to better know ourselves when we disagree or agree with others in conversation.

---

[1] Because of my cultural and familial 'givens' this example is, and most of the examples in the book are, decidedly, but not exclusively, "United States-centric". Iraqi citizens might explore this question about the March 19, 2003 attacks on their country. I encourage readers to come up with relevant, meaningful examples of their own.

[2] Merton, Thomas. "The Inner Experience." *Thomas Merton: Spiritual Master.* Ed. Lawrence S. Cunningham. Mahwah NJ: Paulist, 1992, p. 295.

[3] Wilber, Ken. *Integral Spirituality: A Startling New Role for Religion in the Modern and Postmodern World.* Boston: Integral-Shambhala, 2006, p. 277.

[4] Culture – including national, religious, local, organizational and familial, among others, is a significant breeding ground for "talking points." Members of a large or small group with shared values and desires often embrace the language that their given structure provides. It is possible to do this habitually and unconsciously, as well as intentionally.

[5] If we are fortunate to develop in more or less healthy ways, we begin to question what has been and is given and see how it holds up when compared and contrasted with our own direct experience of the world and the givens and direct experiences of others.

2.

## Who (You Think) You Are in Conversation:
## Part 2 – Within & Beyond Culture

We continue here Chapter One's exploration of ourselves and our worldviews – those values, beliefs, biases and experiences that inform the lenses through which we see and interpret life. In Chapter One we noted the often invisible influence of culture – those 'givens' into which we are born, and which inform our earliest years; here we'll zoom in and explore some other significant influences both beyond and within the impact of culture.

A short list includes genetics (nature), parenting (nurture), personality, health, trauma, multiple intelligences (developmental lines), tendencies concerning the qualities of feminine/masculine, interior/exterior, individual/collective, and Shadow. To the extent that we are aware of, choose to explore, and intentionally develop any of these, we will be more or less knowledgeable about 'who we (think we) are'. What follows is a brief overview of each.

*Genetics/Nature*

Each of us is given by our biological parents the coding for a set of traits, tendencies and possibilities – from physical appearance to various aptitudes. These include our height, body type, hair and eye colors, skin pigmentation, various aptitudes – like academic, athletic or musical prowess, and various predispositions as well: we may carry certain genes that make us more or less susceptible to specific diseases or issues. No one of these creates our destiny, but some of them carry significant influence regarding how others see and treat us, and how we feel about ourselves. Our increasing knowledge of epigenetics, beyond the scope of this book, points to both how much we do, and do not yet know in this area.

*Parenting/Nurture*

Both our culture and our parents provide us with immediate feedback regarding how our nature manifests. Our parents and other influential adults within the context of the larger culture(s) that influence them, provide us with an early view of life that may be more or less (in)accurate and (un)healthy, and which we may embrace, rebel against, or both. If we behave within the acceptable parameters, our journey may be somewhat smooth; if we fall behind or move beyond what the culture and our parents provide and expect, our journey may be tumultuous.

*Personality*

Models of personality (e.g. the Enneagram, Myers-Briggs, etc.) abound and can be helpful – especially when engaged in order to understand ourselves, and not to try to predict or judge ourselves or others. One view of personality is that it emerges through the strategies we engage as children in order to survive, cope, and thrive in our family (and culture) of origin. Often, some of the things that serve us as children are no longer necessary or helpful in adulthood, and if we can recognize them, we can thank them and let them go as we develop. More about this below, in Shadow.

*Health and Trauma*

It is easy for some of us to take good health for granted; it is often only when our sense of wellbeing is "interrupted" by illness or injury that we recognize or remember how it felt to be symptom-free. Serious, persistent health issues and any form of trauma at any age may teach us about vulnerability, mortality, resilience, compassion and hope, as well as about anger, resentment, and despair. Our parents' and other caregivers' attitudes, as well as the culture at large, often carry powerful messages – helpful or hurtful, true or unfounded, about various types of illness and trauma. Our childhood broken arm, and our parents' responses to it – whether we fell from a tree, down the stairs or in the athletic arena, may have any one of various influences on our life moving forward. If we're met with care, compassion, comfort and love, we may openly continue to explore and play – albeit perhaps with some learning from the fall. If we're met with fear, anger and blame, we may shut down and avoid any further exploration or play in which injury is possible. Lives lived in open exploration and with a sense of play feel very different than those lived in fear and with blame.

*Multiple Intelligences/Lines of Development*

Decades of research confirm our ability to develop through intelligences such as linguistic, logical-mathematical, interpersonal, moral, kinesthetic, musical, emotional, spiritual and cognitive, among others. We may become highly developed in one or more of these, less so in others. To make things even more interesting, there is not necessarily a correlation between what we're good at and what we enjoy. To point to obvious examples, my love of music does not necessarily translate into making my living as a musician, or even singing in tune – as is true with my love of a given sport, craft or other discipline.

*Feminine and Masculine Energies*

One way to speak about feminine and masculine energies (as opposed to biological females and males) is that healthy women and men can develop a balance of and comfort with the tendencies toward communion, compassion and mercy – traditionally considered feminine traits, and tendencies toward agency, wisdom and justice – considered masculine traits.[1] As our species continues to recognize homosexual, bisexual, transgender, and heterosexual orientations, the ability to embrace and balance feminine and masculine energies not only remains valid, but may actually deepen. Imagine human beings with increasingly balanced access to healthy communion, agency, compassion, wisdom, mercy and justice.

*Interior/Exterior, Individual/Collective*

Our ongoing attempts to understand our human and other-than-human experience fall into four basic elements – interior, exterior, individual and collective. Ken Wilber's 1995 *Sex, Ecology, Spirituality* introduced us to this "quadrants" model. Here's an example using Habitat for Humanity, whose mission is to "bring people together to build homes, communities and hope."[2]

- The interior-individual refers to an individual's *values and beliefs* that everyone should have a decent place to live, perhaps based in justice, mercy, love or compassion (i.e. interior – within the individual, and *not observable*).
- The exterior-individual refers to the actual behaviors, the observable manifestation of the interior values – signing up to volunteer, carrying lumber, swinging a hammer (i.e. *observable* exterior individual behavior).
- The interior-collective refers to the *shared* beliefs: in this case the mission and vision of the *organization,* excerpted above, the shared belief that it's valuable to "bring people together to build homes, communities and hope" (i.e. interior to and shared within the group).
- The exterior-collective refers to the literal, observable systems, processes and infrastructure that gets the people and material together on time, and assigns roles and actually builds homes, including the website (i.e. observable collective processes, systems, infrastructure).

Anecdotal evidence suggests that each of us tends to favor one or two of these quadrants, ignore one or two, and have varying levels of competence in each of them. Here's an oversimplified summary: if I spend a lot of time "in my head" perhaps I favor the interior-individual; if I'm "action-oriented" and love "doing," I might favor the exterior-individual; if I'm primarily concerned with how everyone is, I might be leaning toward the interior-collective; and if I see myself as a "big-picture" person who "connects the dots," the exterior-collective might be my favorite.

Learning what I favor or ignore and how competent I am in each of these areas can serve as a great checklist (at the very least) for assessing what parts of my life I'm tuned into, what I might be ignoring, and how I tend to address opportunities, problems and change – in conversation and elsewhere.

*Shadow*

Finally, Shadow refers to those traits we repress because our culture or family frowned upon them – what it was not okay to feel, be or do when we were young. In any conversation, if unaware of what we have repressed, we may feel a disproportionate reaction when we notice it in someone else: *I'm* not angry! *You, and everyone like you,* are angry! Bringing our unconscious Shadow into consciousness is an essential step toward wholeness.

~

Yikes. Amid this complexity, it's impressive that we can have any civil conversations, especially when we disagree. Why even bother? One reason is, in David Whyte's words, "The conversation *is* the relationship" in any sustainable, authentic exchange. And while we are focusing on verbal conversation here, the nuances of true conversation transcend and include what we say, as we are asked to "back them words up, pardner," "put our money where our mouth is," and "walk our talk," among other annoying, relevant clichés.

So, before we've even touched on the requisite skills and characteristics of civil, open, honest, and even productive conversation, it's clear that communicating authentically is not for the faint of heart, or the feints of self-knowing and authentic curiosity. No quick fix or magic potion works. We have to do the work, which takes time. Exploring and *engaging* any one of the *italicized* subheads above is a step in a good direction.

## Within and Beyond Culture

Three ways you can engage the *subheads:*

1. Explore and engage a subhead that feels easiest – most accessible to *you.*

2. Explore and engage one that seems most important to you.

3. Explore and engage what you know will be challenging. Then get curious about why you chose as you did.

Finally, and this will resurface in subsequent chapters, complement any work you do with getting to know yourself better with a sense of *not knowing*, especially, but not only with regard to what we call the self. Not knowing is the core of ongoing learning, growth and development. As soon as we "know for sure," we close to other possibilities. Hold your knowing lightly. Stay open.

~

In Chapter Three we'll explore the practice of recognizing and suspending preconceptions, judgments and assumptions in conversation.

---

[1] A case can be made that these feminine and masculine tendencies are themselves culture-based/created. Our focus here is on our awareness of the discrete traits themselves – communion, agency, justice, mercy, wisdom, compassion, etc. and not their historical sources.

[2] https://www.habitat.org/

~

**Selected resources:**

- Among many personality type systems, I'll mention three: the Enneagram; Myers-Briggs; and DiSC. Of the three, I have the most training in, and tend to use the Enneagram. If you'd like to explore it, visit https://www.enneagraminstitute.com/type-descriptions or https://www.enneagramworldwide.com/tour-the-nine-types/ and read the details of the types – noting what feels familiar and unfamiliar. My personal bias, based on how I tend to learn, is not taking online assessments (free samples or paid full versions) until you have some sense of your type. Read and feel into what feels accurate for you. Then the assessments might be helpful. Plenty of books are available as well.

- One of my favorite authors on Howard Gardner's work with multiple intelligences is Thomas Armstrong. His *You're Smarter Than You Think* is an accessible and fun volume that parents and children can use together. http://www.institute4learning.com/resources/.

- For a brief overview of developmental lines, interiors, exteriors, individuals and collectives (and the rest of his AQAL model), see Ken Wilber's *The Integral Vision* (2007) a "pocket edition" of which was released in November 2018. If you'd like a volume that provides both theory and an approach to practice, see *Integral Life Practice* (Wilber, Patten, et. al., 2010). Many additional titles by Ken Wilber are available.

- For an exploration of how culture, illness and trauma can intersect, see Lewis Mehl-Medrona's *Coyote Wisdom: The Power of Story in Healing.* Rochester, VT: Bear & Company, 2005 (among other titles by the author); Gabor Maté's *When the Body Says No: Exploring the Stress-Disease Connection.* Hoboken, NJ: Wiley & Sons, 2003; and Bessel van der Kolk's *The Body Keeps the Score: Brain, Mind and Body in the Healing of Trauma.* New York: Penguin, 2014.

- For an overview of Shadow that includes a perspective on how a culture can have a collective Shadow, see my own "Revisiting

'Donald Trump, Collective American Shadow, and "the Better Angels of Our Nature"'" (2018), at https://reggiemarra.com/. Also, sixty-five essays provide a multi-perspective overview of Shadow in *Meeting the Shadow,* edited by Connie Zweig and Jeremiah Abrams (1991).

# 3.

## Recognizing and Suspending Preconceptions, Judgments and Assumptions

So, yes, culture, in the broadest view that includes race,[1] ethnicity, gender, orientation, religion, etc., along with genetics, parenting, personal experience, health, trauma, propensity to learn, and many other factors, leads us to hold certain preconceptions, judgments and assumptions about ourselves, others and the world. Some of these can be helpful in navigating our everyday lives. Choosing to assume that many motor vehicle drivers are somewhat distracted (not necessarily, or just, with phones) by life in general can keep us safe – and both minimize the chances of overreacting when someone is careless and enhance the feelings of joy and gratitude when someone is unexpectedly courteous on the road. Choosing to assume that the walkway and road may be icy after an evening of freezing drizzle can be useful.

The most important words in the examples above are "choosing to assume." We don't *know* which drivers are distracted, but if we choose to recognize the possibility that many, including ourselves, are, this choice allows us to be more prepared and less reactive – sparing both us and other drivers *from us* when someone is careless, and ridiculously grateful when someone is attentive or courteous. We don't *know* which stretch of pavement is icy, but recognizing the probability of icy patches leads us to walk or drive with more care. An *intentional* choice to assume, while it can be harmful or helpful, is easier to eliminate or embrace once we see the harm or help.

What we're concerned with here are those preconceptions, judgments and assumptions that we haven't chosen intentionally: more often than not, *they have chosen us. They have us,*[2] we don't know it, and we think we're seeing and hearing that other person, and the rest of the world, as he, she or it is, when we're actually seeing and hearing who and as we are, filtered through all of those lenses noted in this chapter's first sentence and throughout the previous two chapters.

This is not a new idea. Versions of it have been around for millennia: *stop looking through that glass darkly,* and *get that plank out of your eye!* Still, when we look at or listen to most 'conversations' in which people are disagreeing on issues across political and other divides – whether in traditional media, on social media or in person, and whether they're elected officials, news commentators, celebrities (or some combination thereof), social critics, 'thought leaders' or just ordinary folks, most of them, and most of us, behave as though we are certain that 1) we see things as things are, 2) we are correct, and 3) our "opponent" is wrong.

Now, I hope, the significance of the first two chapters' explorations of who we (think we) are in conversation is more apparent. Before we have any real chance of opening up and seeing and hearing another human being in conversation with even a basic level of authenticity and integrity, we need to have some idea of how our glass is dark, how dark it is, and what the dimensions and composition are of that plank, beam, log or speck that's lodged in our own eye(s).

One way into this is to gain some clarity on a preconception, judgment or assumption we have, or that has us: *why do we have it, or does it have us, and what's the impact of the having?* Byron

Katie suggests asking ourselves these questions:[3]

1. Is it true?
2. Can I absolutely know that it's true?
3. How do I react when I think that thought (preconception, judgment or assumption)?
4. Who would I be without this thought (preconception, judgment or assumption)?

That fourth question asks us to explore what it might be like to suspend our preconceptions, judgments and assumptions in conversation (or forever) – even if they can be proven true (right now). There's more to this process (see link below), but these four questions, engaged authentically, can open some doors.

If I enter a conversation with strong beliefs about the superiority of the Yankees or the Red Sox (just my choosing sports and those two teams as examples tells you something about me and my cultural 'givens'), liberals or conservatives, gays or straights, wisdom or compassion, justice or mercy, etc., my chances for authentic, open dialogue will be limited or enhanced by the extent to which I voluntarily, accurately and thoroughly recognize, investigate and suspend – or permanently let go when appropriate, those historically given beliefs and assumptions (aka scripts, tapes, films, stories, narratives, etc.) that hold me. This choosing to recognize and authentically investigate, may, of course, lead to my choosing to continue to embrace a belief, but now it will be a belief that I intentionally hold or have, and not one that holds or has me.

This is difficult, essential work if we are to speak from our hearts with, and deeply listen to, each other.

## That Log in Your Eye!

One way to approach this work right now:

- (Re)read Chapter One and return to the six bulleted responses to the events of September 11, 2001 on pages 10 & 11 (or choose any other disaster or tragedy about which there exist disparate responses or opinions). For each, go a little deeper with the second reflection question posed there (*What is it about you and your worldview such that you react as you do?*): note your reaction to each of the six points, and explore the preconceptions, judgments and assumptions you have, or that have you, that lead to your reaction.

Do this not to prove yourself "right" or "wrong" but to explore and get to know yourself better.

~

In Chapter Four, we'll consider the effects of avoiding insults, labels and/or sweeping generalizations in conversation.

---

[1] Disagreements exist concerning whether race is a social construct or an empirically measurable trait. Social construct, measurable trait or something else, race historically, perceptually and pragmatically has *de facto* impact on our lives.

[2] For more on the idea of having assumptions vs. being had by them, see Robert Kegan's and Lisa Laskow Lahey's *Immunity to Change: How to Overcome It and Unlock the Potential in Yourself and Your Organization.* http://mindsatwork.com/

[3] From "The Work" by Byron Katie. For some context, and a deeper dive into each question, visit http://thework.com/en/do-work.  See also her *Loving What Is: Four Questions That Can Change Your Life.* New York: Harmony, 2002.

# Part Two

*Honoring Facts and Identifying Opinions –
Really? Will That Hold Up in Court
or in the Laboratory?*

# 4.

## Avoiding Labels, Insults and Sweeping Generalizations

Most of us experience our first tree at a young age. Depending upon our location, how old we are, whom we're with, and our sense of adventure, this first tree experience may be a moment of sensory wonder or a casual, soon forgotten encounter. The same can be said about most initial meetings – a river, a bird, or a mountain; a book, a guitar or a painting; a train, plane or a motorcycle; a loved one, a friend, a parent or child.

Soon enough, even with that last group, the label – "tree," "guitar," "train," or "mom" replaces the actual thing or person, which or whom we no longer experience with any sense of curiosity or wonder. We "kind of" know what or who each is. We use labels and generalizations as a matter of course, and when we dislike or disapprove of someone or something we use insulting labels and sweeping generalizations. Sometimes the labels are targeted and specific and sometimes they're more general.[1]

Imagine individuals who regularly use labels like "fake," "failing," or "not very good" to refer to people and organizations they disagree with or do not like – especially in situations in which they seem to have neither the specific information nor the ability to articulate what it is they really want to say, and "great" to refer to what they believe in and what they want others to embrace. In each of these cases – the negative labeling of others and the positive labeling of themselves or their ideas, the labels are devoid of any real meaning. They are unsubstantiated insults and praise.

Were these individuals, or anyone who uses language in this way, able to point to concrete evidence, *facts* that warrant and support descriptors like "fake," "failing" or "great" (that last one being the most subjective and most challenging to support with evidence), their words might carry some weight. Again, in the absence of such evidence, the first two words, as they use them, are simply insulting and the third is simply, and often provably, grandiose.

Now consider other words like *conservative, liberal, progressive, socialist, feminist, elite, fascist* and any number of other labels that attempt to capture ethnic, national, sexual, skin pigmentation and other group classifications. Notice which of these substitute labels you're sure you understand accurately. Once you've done that, get curious about what you might be missing each time you rely on the label rather than doing the work that is necessary to truly and deeply understand a concept – or another human being, group of human beings, or, as we began with above, a *tree*. "Tree" is a far cry from the living, breathing, reaching, rooted life form it represents, as "mom" does not quite capture the complexity of that woman who carried us and ushered us into the world.

Yes, it can be convenient, efficient and harmless to use labels and generalizations in our day-to-day communication, especially with people we know and in contexts in which conflict and disagreement are absent. We (think we) know what our neighbor means when she sees us on that first sunny, blue-skied, 65-degree day after a long winter, and says, "Beautiful day!" Or do we? Perhaps she just got engaged, won the lottery, her cancer is in remission, or she's on her way to the airport for a much anticipated vacation. And regardless of what it is that motivates her utterance of these words, there's no harm and perhaps a lot of good in our responding with something like "Yes, it is – enjoy!" – even if we have no idea why she says this, and perhaps, it's a beautiful day for us simply *because* she says this.

When any one of us utters words like *liberal* or *conservative* in an otherwise friendly conversation, absent any further elucidation the words have only limited meaning outside the context of where the speaker and the listener self-identify on the political spectrum (and on how accurate their self-identities are). If Bernie Sanders criticizes someone or something as having a liberal bias, it arouses more interest than if Mitch McConnell says it. If McConnell criticizes a conservative bias, that's unusual; for Sanders, not so much. Where any one of us stands on the political spectrum *and* on specific issues controls how we use those two labels. The same is true with any label or generalization we use outside the realm of politics. If I am ignorant of where I stand, what my view is, and what informs my view (the focus of Chapters One, Two and Three), not only will my labels and generalizations usually do more harm than good, they will do so from a place of ignorance.

One's level of formal education, number of degrees and the alleged prestige of schools attended neither preclude nor necessarily lead to the ignorant use of labels and generalizations. A terminal degree *may* narrow and limit one's view even as it deepens knowledge and insight in its field of focus; having no degree *may* limit academic orientation or knowledge *and* invite and allow curiosity beyond what academia finds important. Ignorance of self and self-knowing are equal opportunity characteristics.

> Indelibservatarians Untie![2]

One way to explore this right now:
1. Make a list of things – in your personal/professional life and in society – that you would like to change or see changed.

2. Repeat #1 for things that you would like to keep as they are.

3. Define *liberal* as you understand the word, and provide a few examples of people and positions on issues for which the word feels accurate to you.

4. Repeat #3 using the word *conservative*.

5. Based on your responses to 1-4, in general, and for specific issues, how do the words *liberal* and *conservative* apply to *you*, if (you think) they do at all?

    a. What impact, if any, does this exercise have on how you feel about the words *liberal* and *conservative?*

    b. What impact, if any, does it have on how you feel about yourself?

~

In Chapter Five, we'll explore the difference between opinion and fact (something with which many readers may have thought they were done). In Chapter Six, we'll take a look at how we might limit or replace our labels and generalizations with learning how to provide specific, factual and preferably personal examples to support our opinions.

---

[1] It's important not to confuse stereotypical labels, characterizations and generalizations with the often expansive, clarifying power of metaphor. *Intention* has an essential role here. For more on the presence of metaphor in language, see, among others, George Lakoff and Mark Johnson's *Metaphors We Live By*.

[2] Yes, deliberately transposed, and "Indelibservatarians" (spoiler alert) refers to independents, liberals, conservatives and libertarians. But you knew that.

# 5.

## Getting Clear on and Honoring the Difference Between Opinion and Fact

For our purposes, a *fact* is something that competent, disinterested, unattached, "ideal" observers (i.e. those who understand something and have no interest in it other than an honest assessment of its existence and qualities) agree is true.[1] An *opinion* is a statement of how someone interprets, what someone believes and/or how someone feels about something – whether that 'something' is a fact or another opinion.

Many of us were introduced to the difference between opinion and fact somewhere in middle-to-late childhood or early adolescence. Many of us seem to have forgotten this difference or have chosen to behave as though it's not really important. My sense of this (i.e. my opinion) is that a variety of factors contribute to this forgetting or this choice. Here are a few:

- *A genuine inability or disingenuous refusal to differentiate* what happened *and* my interpretation of what happened. E.g. after the collision of two cars at the four-way-stop intersection, one *fact* is that the cars made contact and sustained damage. Often, the drivers will have different interpretations (opinions) of that collision and what caused it, and will state them as 'facts': "She rolled through the stop sign… I looked both ways… He was looking at his phone…" While any one of these may be factual, absent consistent eyewitness accounts and/or clear traffic cam footage, they represent the opinions of the drivers involved.

- *A tendency to accept as true or factual what one hears, reads or views in various media* – whether television, radio, podcast, book, magazine, newspaper, etc., or from various 'authorities' or 'experts' – whether elected officials, 'celebrities', 'thought leaders', or religious leaders. We tend to do this when the medium or 'expert' reinforces or confirms what we already believe.[2] This tendency applies to sacred scripture and national constitutions and charters as well. It is useful – in the best meaning of that word, perhaps essential, to explore iterations of stories beyond our trusted sources in order to get closer to 'the truth'. Here are several useful questions:
    - How often do you seek and/or uncover a voice or iteration from the "other side" that feels closer to 'true' than your more trusted sources provide?
    - If and when this happens, how do you feel about it?
    - What do you do with and about this feeling?

- Often underlying each of these questions is *an inability or refusal to engage honest self-reflection and/or critical thinking:* What would it mean if I discover that I've been wrong *about this* – whatever *this* refers to, or *for years*, or *for decades*? What would it mean if I discover that I've been wrong and I choose to hold on to my wrongness because letting go of my old beliefs is just too painful – more painful than keeping them, as it usually is?

- *Lack of awareness of the impact of myriad cultural and personal influences on how each of us experiences (the moments and events in) his or her life*, as summarized in Chapters One, Two and Three.

- *A relentless commitment to winning an argument, defending habitual thoughts, advocating a view that's in our best interest, or discrediting a view with which we disagree, that scares us, or both.*

One way to move toward differentiating fact and opinion amid disagreement, especially when both or all disagreeing parties are authentically willing to listen and reflect (yes, that is possible) is to try to find what Ken Wilber has called *orienting generalizations* – points of general agreement that disagreeing parties may find if they step far enough back from the immediate issue or conflict.[3]

Consider *your* views on gun rights and legislation, abortion, health care, race, public education, income inequality, ongoing war and minimum wage, among other issues. Imagine what orienting generalization(s) or larger points of agreement you and an 'opponent' might find in the 'what' and 'how' of resolving these, or any local or personal issues. One way into this is for each party to get clear on and clearly state what he or she really wants and needs – the desire(s) and/or the need(s) behind my position in this conversation: *What do I really want/need in and from this conversation – in the short term? In the long term?*

Notice *your own* stances and biases as you do this. Tune in as best you can to what is fact and what is opinion. As best you can, zero in on *your* ability to differentiate and define events or issues and your interpretations of them. Note what 'authoritative' sources, if any, you rely on for 'facts'. Get intimate with your level of engagement with critical thought and/or self-reflection: one way to begin is to interrogate any longstanding belief you hold. Identify the cultural influences of your childhood and your current life. Note the extent to which you want to win, defend or discredit in conversation, as opposed to acknowledge, understand or learn.

As you can see, or may be beginning to see, the obstacles to open, civil, healing conversation that leads to learning and growth for the parties involved can be significant – as can be the learning and growth themselves, and therein lies the value, the reason to try. Imagine walking away from a disagreement (or an agreement) with a renewed sense of respect for 'the other', and with a broader, deeper view of an issue, oneself, the other, or the world at large.

Our goal in this, and each successive chapter is to provide a basic tool kit that facilitates doing the work necessary for anyone who truly wants to engage in discourse in ways that broaden and deepen understanding of self, other human beings and viewpoints – whether or not any disagreement is resolved.

## Beware the Expert & Thought Leader

Some ways to explore fact and opinion right now:

1. Uncover at least one *opinion* you've held onto and presented as fact for at least a year, and get as clear as you can on why you did, or are still doing, this. Do this with a desire for cleaning up your views, and not with a feeling of guilt or shame.

2. Take an honest look at whom you trust as sources of news, and explore how you might allow other sources and perspectives in – whether or not you shift your view. The goal is to listen and understand even amid disagreement.

3. To what extent have you been, and are you currently, open to honest self-reflection and critical thinking? What issues would it upset or 'terrify' you to discover you've been 'wrong' – or even only partially 'right' about?

4. How aware are you of the cultural, personal and experiential 'input' that contributes to your current worldview? Get clear

on what areas of your 'givens' and your experience you have genuinely explored, and what areas you have not.

5. How open do you tend to be in conversation, and especially in disagreement? How do your desires to win, defend and discredit match up with your desires to learn, understand and grow?

Be kind to yourself as you explore these questions.

~

In Chapter Six we'll take a look at how we might limit or replace our labels and generalizations with specific, factual and preferably personal examples to support our opinions.

---

[1] We could easily open and jump into a deep rabbit hole concerning exactly what the standard is for words like "competent." We won't do that here.

[2] Much has been written about *confirmation bias*. E.g.:
https://www.britannica.com/science/confirmation-bias
https://www.psychologytoday.com/us/blog/science-choice/201504/what-is-confirmation-bias

[3] Wilber, Ken. *Sex, Ecology, Spirituality: The Spirit of Evolution.* Boston: Shambhala, 1995 (xiii-ix).

# 6.

## Antidotes for Generalizations, Labels and Insults: Get Specific, Factual, Personal & Aware of Others

To get started, please select one of the following statements that is consistent with your views, or come up with another statement that captures how you view one of these, or some other issue:

- Mainstream media has a consistent, dangerous liberal bias.
- Fox News, a mouthpiece for conservative views and especially Donald Trump, is unfair and unbalanced.
- The Patient Protection and Affordable Care Act made health insurance unaffordable for many people.
- The United States' struggles with public education, health care, income inequality, domestic violence and ongoing war in the Middle East, contrasted with other post-industrial democratic nations, are embarrassing and have nothing to do with world leadership or greatness.
- The United States is the greatest, wealthiest, most powerful nation in the history of the planet.

More personal statements work as well. The above capture some of the 'factual' tone that is prevalent amid exchanges in much political discourse. I recommend your working with something that's important to you. What follows is my modeling one way to work with generalizations, labels and insults.

> I often observe otherwise good, intelligent, competent [my opinions and judgments] human beings speaking through frustration, anger, resentment or fear [i.e. speaking emotionally,[1] despite their capacity for rationality] about something, and resorting to sweeping generalizations, faulty reasoning (it happened to me, so it must be true for everyone, or vice versa), and/or insult in disagreement with others. *Perhaps the best place to witness this is on social media / where political and celebrity scoundrels and ne'er-do-wells / fire off their (not so) clever jibes and partial truths, / which their friends and followers ingest and regurgitate like so much nutritionally devoid vomit.*

Let's break down that *italicized* sentence:

- *"Perhaps the best place to witness this is on social media"* forms my opinion – which is 'truthful', i.e. I really do believe social media are among the best places to observe this phenomenon ('truthful' as opposed to 'The Truth', i.e. empirically provable, which we'll address in Chapter 14).
- *"[W]here political and celebrity scoundrels and ne'er-do-wells"* provides intentional generalization and insults.
- *"[F]ire off their (not so) clever jibes and partial truths"* are my judgments about and characterizations of what they do.
- *"[W]hich their friends and followers ingest and regurgitate like so much nutritionally devoid vomit"* was the first image and simile that my mind produced; its tastelessness (no pun intended) corresponds with my experience of these social media exchanges.

That sentence was fun to write, and it generalizes and insults. Here's the beginning of a more specific, personal exploration of what I truly want to express, and *one way* I might go about expressing it:

FACT: Some politicians and celebrities, among other folks, generalize and insult each other on social media. That's not all they do, and they're not the only ones – but they do this.

FEELING: I personally resent their doing this (even those with whom I might agree on an issue) for a variety of reasons, including, but not limited to, these three beliefs:

- In my experience of the world, no significant personal, national or global problem has been resolved by a tit-for-tat exchange of lies, partial truths or insults (via social media or any other means).
- I want my elected officials to spend their time addressing issues that impact tens of millions of people every day, rather than playing "I-got-you-last" in public or on social media (even if they have a staff member playing for them).
- Technology is neutral: the invention of the wheel facilitated transportation *and* allows us to run over people and deliver car bombs. The internet can be used by the local soup kitchen *and* the local hate group. Elected officials and members of our celebrity cult(ure) can choose not to use social media, and/or change how they use it.

OBSERVATION: Many of us simply share what we read or hear without 1) confirming its accuracy, or 2) thinking for ourselves about the issue – allowing Merton's "anonymous authority of the collectivity" or Wilber's "structure"[2] to speak through and for us. It can be time consuming *and* quite valuable to check for accuracy and critically think about an issue before repeating what someone else has written or said.

BELIEF: Technological advances that quicken and mobilize communication have diverse, positive impacts *and* contribute to the deterioration of language skills and depth of communication (ask any language arts teacher who was in the classroom before smart phones, and is still there now). Something gets lost in the move from spoken, in-person conversation, to phone, video, email, texting and social media exchanges. I write this as someone who earns a good part of my living via video conversations, not as a technophobe. Accurate tornado and active shooter alerts save lives; inaccurate accusations, generalizations and insults ruin lives. Both are true. *Skillful means* is a universally applicable tool.

These will suffice.

Here's that sentence again, without italics and slashes: "Perhaps the best place to witness this is on social media, where political and celebrity scoundrels and ne'er-do-wells fire off their (not so) clever jibes and partial truths, which their friends and followers ingest and regurgitate like so much nutritionally devoid vomit." The above process provides me with some clarity about what I truly wanted to express. It's something very close to this:

> *I worry for my family, my friends, my fellow citizens and myself, and I resent those elected officials and celebrities who insult each other, state opinions as facts (whether through vincible or invincible ignorance or intentional manipulation – each of which is problematic), and behave in ways that loving parents and competent teachers do not tolerate from their children and students – at any age.*

Note the respective impacts of these two statements. The latter attempts to differentiate fact, opinion, observation and belief, and expresses a very personal worry that underlies its position. The move from the former to the latter is the *beginning* of a thoughtful process – one that the pace and limitations of social media, and even much broadcast and print media, neither allow nor encourage, and one that is difficult, if not impossible to engage in the absence of ongoing self-reflection and critical thought turned both inward and outward – preferably by all parties involved.

One way to get specific, factual, personal and aware of others:

What follows is a synopsis of my view of 'healthcare' in the United States. I provide it here as a model of an intentional attempt to express an opinion that is specific, personal, factual and aware of others, and *not* as an argument for my particular view:

> When I first became aware, circa 1977-78, that millions of United States citizens did not have health insurance or access to affordable healthcare, I was making about $9,500 a year as a twenty-four year-old Catholic high school teacher and basketball coach in New York, and had basic health insurance through my job, with a small monthly premium withheld. My response then was that I'd gladly pay a reasonable amount more each month, assuming that all insured Americans would do the same, if it meant that all Americans would have access to affordable health care.
>
> No U.S. Congress majority or President in either party took any substantial action to address this issue until Hillary Clinton moved with it during her tenure as First Lady. It ended badly for her and her husband. The federal government and the insurance and pharmaceutical industries had no discernible desire to make sure citizens in the U.S. had access to affordable, competent healthcare.
>
> Barack Obama made it a priority and the 2010 Patient Protection and Affordable Care Act came into being – criticized by progressives as not going far enough, and by conservatives as the socialization of America.
>
> Between 1996 and 2000, and then from 2013 on, I paid insurance premiums out of pocket. By 2016 the rates had risen to the point where it made sense for me to gamble that I would not get sick or hurt (i.e. not have health insurance) rather than to continue gambling that I would, and throwing good money after bad. So for 2016, 2017, 2018 and the first four months of 2019, I had no health insurance – the cheapest rates (least coverage and highest deductible) in Connecticut for a white male my age (62-64 in those three years), which had nothing to do with my lifestyle, health, or personal and family medical history, ranged from 12% to just under 18% of my gross income, before deductibles, which were another $6k annually. Those rates, as a percentage of

income, also meant I was exempt from any penalty for not having coverage.

Twice during those three years I paid for an annual physical exam out of pocket, which cost me somewhere between $28,000 and $30,000 less than if I had paid insurance premiums. In mid-2019 I became eligible for Medicare, which both alleviated some problems and created some new ones.

I have been blessed with relatively healthy genes, and intentionally care for my physical, mental, emotional and spiritual health. The Patient Protection and Affordable Care Act of 2010 allowed insurance companies to significantly raise my premiums, not because of who I am or my medical history, but because of their sense of a nonexistent average white male in his 50's and 60's.[3] It also provided access to affordable healthcare for millions of Americans who had not previously had access.

All of this considered and written, I supported and support the Patient Protection and Affordable Care Act as an important *first step* (which is how President Obama described it) in reforming the pharmaceutical-medical-insurance industry in the United States. At the same time it helped tens of millions of U.S. citizens get access to affordable health care, it allowed insurance companies to price me and others out of the market at a time I was fortunate enough to be in good health.

## Specific, Factual, Personal & Aware

Your work now (should you accept this mission) is to formulate your own specific, factual, personal and aware-of-others statement on this issue, or any other issue of your choosing. Get to the heart of your beliefs and stance on what matters to you in a specific, factual, personal and aware-of-others way.

~

In Chapter Seven we'll explore the usefulness of curiosity, knowing and not knowing.

[1] This is not a criticism of emotion; a balance of emotion and reason tends to be more integrated. We want to utilize our brain function optimally – instinct, emotion *and* reason.

[2] See Chapter One, p. 4.

[3] That's just my geographic, age, race and gender version. Many people had it worse than I did and have it worse than I do. Statistical averages for nonexistent individuals across race, gender, geography and age allow and invite large entities in both public and private sectors to ignore the existence of unique individuals. Such averages or norms can be useful on occasion – such as in recognizing lifestyle and genetic markers for disease, but even there, that "average" person simply doesn't exist and doesn't capture the reality of any real human being.

# Part Three

*Learning Intentionally – How Do You Want to Be, and What Do You Hope for, in this Conversation?*

# 7.

## Curiosity, Knowing and Not Knowing on the Path of Learning

Chapters One, Two and Three briefly allude to the importance of "not knowing." Chapter Two explicitly states: *Not knowing is the core of ongoing learning, growth and development. As soon as we "know for sure," we close to other possibilities. Hold your knowing lightly. Stay open.* Depending upon your worldview and how you interpret the phrase, *not knowing* as a path of learning may sound like common sense – or like idiocy.

Students of Korean Zen Master Seung Sahn[1] (1927-2004), among others, might readily embrace this language and approach, while students of conventional medicine (or engineering or climate change, etc.) might be more apt to prefer as much knowing as possible in order to do more good than harm in their respective endeavors. To be fair, most honest, well-meaning human beings prefer to have appropriate knowledge before making choices or taking action in their personal and professional lives, where "appropriate" means relevant, adequate,[2] useful, kind and balanced. Ideally, appropriate knowledge refers to both the exterior world – what we might know about practical applications of biology, chemistry and physics, for example, before performing surgery, building a bridge or proliferating fluorocarbons, and to the interior world – what we might know about ourselves – the worldview and lenses through which we experience, interpret and respond to life.

The relationship between *knowing* and *not knowing* that we're moving toward here asks us to return to our differentiating fact and opinion, or, put differently, to look carefully at our human tendency to blend what we know as fact with our immediate interpretation of what the fact might *mean* in the moment and for and in the future. A common parable with which you may already be familiar makes this point:

> In olden times a farmer was told by his neighbors how lucky he was because he owned a prized horse. He replied, "Maybe I'm lucky; maybe I'm not." When the horse jumped the fence and galloped away, the neighbors told the farmer how unlucky he was. His reply: "Maybe I'm unlucky; maybe I'm not." Several days later the horse returned, accompanied by three wild horses. "You're so lucky," the neighbors told him. "Maybe I am; maybe I'm not," he said. The farmer's oldest son fell while riding one of the wild horses, and broke his leg, and the neighbors told the farmer how unlucky this was. "Maybe so, maybe not," came his reply, and when the army came through to conscript the oldest son in each family to go to war, they did not take the farmer's son because of the broken leg. The neighbors commented and the farmer replied.

When I shared that story in a high school in Tucson in 1995, one student said that something like that had happened to him. He explained that he broke his leg in a football game; in the hospital doctors noticed something about the break and did tests that revealed evidence of early-stage bone marrow cancer for which he underwent treatment and went into remission. He now credits breaking his leg, which when it happened was traumatic and felt 'unlucky' at best, with finding out about the cancer sooner rather than later. What at first felt like a devastating blow to his football career and his dreams of playing in college, subsequently felt like a "lucky break" that may have prolonged – even saved, his life.

Simply put, we interpret and give meaning before we know what some event or moment truly means. Our ability to *know* what's truly knowable about something, and to be comfortable "resting" in *not knowing* what is not yet ours to know allows us to remain authentically *curious* and open to learning. As we engage in conversation with someone with whom we disagree (or agree), the extent to which we recognize and acknowledge how much we truly know and don't know about ourselves, the other, and the content of the conversation will strongly influence, if not completely determine, each party's openness to and opportunity for growth and learning.

Such recognition, acknowledgment and openness requires and cultivates vulnerability – not in the sense of weakness or being overly susceptible to harm, injury or loss, but rather in the sense of showing up fully and authentically, hiding nothing and trusting – even in the face of fear. How willing and able is each of us, in our respective roles as parents, children, significant others, students, friends, colleagues and workers – in the broadest sense across industries and professions, to let go, or at least monitor our initial interpretations of any moment, glance, smile, frown, gesture, laugh, phrase – anything at all, and intentionally explore and allow meaning to emerge[3] in increasingly broader and deeper contexts?

At the heart of a willingness to open and not know lies an authentic, playful sense of curiosity – a genuine sense of wonder about the world. This is not the judging curiosity behind, *I'm really curious about why you would do that after the conversation we had last week,* or *I'm curious about what led you to think it was okay to say that out loud in front of everyone,* but rather the often unspoken curiosity about the mystery that is our loved one, a clear night sky, a work of art, or anything that breathes, including ourselves.

~

## Curiosity, Beyond the Myth of the Cat

Several ways to explore curiosity, knowing and not knowing right now:

Select an opinion you hold about an issue that is important to you. It can, but need not, be one of the bullet points on page 3. In the context of the issue, create a short (or long) list for each of the following:

- Things you're sure you *know* about it.
- Things you're sure you *don't know* and about which you have no curiosity.
- Things about which you're genuinely *curious*.

1. For the first bullet, select one of the things you're sure you know and apply Byron Katie's questions from pp. 22-23. Repeat with other items on the list.

2. For the second bullet, explore, as deeply as you dare, what's behind your reluctance to learn more about this issue that's important to you.

3. For the third bullet, select one of the things you're curious about and learn more about it.

4. After you've gone through these steps once, complete this sentence stem: *What I'm beginning to see is* _____. Repeat as needed.

~

In Chapter Eight we'll explore the importance of engaging (listening, speaking and asking) in order to learn, understand and clarify, and not to teach or persuade (unless teaching or persuasion has been agreed upon by participating parties in the conversation).

[1] Among other sources: https://tricycle.org/magazine/master-seung-sahn-1927-2004/

[2] While it may be appropriate, even necessary, in certain circumstances to have *comprehensive* or *exhaustive* knowledge, it is very often appropriate to have *adequate* – sufficient or enough knowledge for what is required or needed, for a particular choice or action in a given moment. The roles of language, belief, interpretation and worldview allow different people at different times to honestly embrace slogans like: *Good is the enemy of great* or *Great is the enemy of good.*

[3] There are times when we don't have the temporal luxury of allowing meaning to emerge – medical emergencies and other literal moments of life and death. That said, these are few and far between for most of us during most of the moments of our lives, especially in conversation.

# 8.

## Conversing in Order to Learn, Understand and Gain Clarity, Rather than Trying to Teach, Persuade or Disprove*

*Conversations in which participants agree that the nature of the discourse involves teaching, persuasion and/or proof or disproof, like formal debate, litigation, scientific research, and some professional trainings are not the focus of this chapter or this book, although parts of this book might serve some of them as well.

Imagine engaging a disagreement (or agreement) with a friend, family member, acquaintance, colleague or stranger with the intention of learning from and more deeply understanding the other's perspective and further clarifying your own. Imagine not being concerned with or interested in trying to convince the other of something, pointing out what he doesn't know or why and how she's wrong, 'winning' in some way or other, or making him or her look bad. Imagine showing up in conversation with authentic curiosity, the ability to listen deeply, and a desire to ask and respond to genuine questions, the only purpose of which is mutual learning, understanding and clarity. *That* does *require imagination,* you may be thinking.

The three general imaginings above are not a prescription for *the right way* to be in conversation. They are, I believe, practical and essential prerequisites if any authentic verbal exchange is to have a chance of evolving beyond the alternating combative monologues, often vitriolic, that masquerade as 'dialogue' or 'conversation' in contemporary public and private life – and they would arguably have something to offer the formal debate, litigation, research and trainings exceptions mentioned above as well.

*Engaging,* as used here refers to listening, speaking and asking questions, again, with the intention to learn, understand and clarify with, from and through an authentically curious and open mind and heart. The curious and open mind helps us inquire, speak and understand accurately and skilfully; the curious and open heart allows us to accept and respect the other, and the common humanity we share.

### One Approach That Helps

A deceptively simple, clarifying question, even more effective when repeated, is something like[1] *When you say \_\_\_\_, what do you really mean by that* or *what does that really mean to* you? I use this type question[2] as part of a writing practice – and it works alone, with a partner or group, and also with coaching clients. For example, I'll write a sentence, or some longer unit of writing and ask myself, *What do I* **mean** *by that?* I'll respond to that question in writing, and then ask again, perhaps with different emphasis, *What do I mean by* **that**? I'll respond again and continue the cycle until I can no longer fine-tune my meaning. Once I get to that point, I may ask, *How does this make me feel?* Depending on my intention, I can then use the same process to inquire into the meaning of my response to that feeling question. If you've never done this, I recommend giving it a try.

To be effective in conversation, the question, *What does that mean?* or *What do you mean by that?* must come from a place of curiosity and with a desire for learning and clarity. There are lots of ways to 'soften' these questions so they're not heard as criticisms (What the %?*@! do you mean?!). Here's one: *The story I'm telling* *myself about what you just said is* _____, *and I'm wondering if that's close to what you really meant. If so, great. If not, what did you mean? I really want us to be on the same page as we move forward* (or something like that).[3]

When it comes to listening through and with an open mind and heart, it's essential to remember the importance of our awareness of the 'lenses'[4] through which we're listening, even with our minds and hearts open. Each of us can open his or her mind and heart. Not every mind or heart is equally open.

I'll leave you with four intentions that I first learned sitting in council[5] when I enacted a Vision Quest in 1998 with Bill Plotkin and the guides at Animas Valley Institute.[6] I believe these intentions can serve anyone, anywhere.

> Speak from your heart.
>
> Listen from, with and through your heart.
>
> Be of lean expression.
>
> Be spontaneous (in the sense of being in the moment and not rehearsing).

### The Story I'm Telling Myself

Several ways to play with understanding, learning and clarifying in conversation:

- Begin exploring your opinions through written expressions followed by the repeating question, "What do I mean by that?" as described above.

- Once you have a feel for that, gently try it out in conversation, asking the other the question in an authentically curious way: *What do you mean by that?*

- Experiment with the four intentions of council: take the time to feel what it feels like to embody each of them (e.g. how does speaking or listening from the heart feel, contrasted with speaking or listening from the head?).

~

In Chapter Nine we'll explore the impact of holding the intention of finding similarities, and not just differences, with those with whom we disagree.

---

[1] I use the phrase "something like" here to emphasize that there is not exactly one correct question to use here. What's important is what the question allows/invites us to do next.

[2] For more on this type of inquiry, perhaps explore proprioceptive writing: http://pwriting.org/. The example above is not intended to represent the teachings of Linda Trichter Metcalf, Tobin Simon, *et. al.*

[3] "The story I'm telling myself…" Thanks to Brett Thomas for sharing this.

[4] See Chapters One, Two and Three to review these lenses.

[5] See *The Way of Council* by Jack Zimmerman in collaboration with Virginia Coyle for a more detailed exploration of these intentions in the context of council (and for more on what *council* refers to).

[6] https://animas.org/

Part Four

*Acknowledging the Forest and Staying on the Path – Wow, You're Human Too!*

# 9.

# Finding Similarities as Well as Differences in Disagreement

Often in disagreement both sides get so caught up in defending their positions and attempting to prove the other wrong in order to 'win' – whatever that might mean, they simply cannot imagine, or aren't interested in speaking about, areas in which their views are similar – or even the same. This is especially true when there's an audience for their exchange. Here are two generic, general and fictional[1] examples of how this can shift, and one "real-life" example in which the similarities, the will to find them, or both seem unattainable for the involved parties:

1. Parties in an environmental dispute might disagree about which groups of flora and fauna are most at risk and how they should be protected. In their focus on *which* and *how*, they fail to notice, or noticing, fail to honor, their shared perspective that all the at-risk plants and animals populate a specific forest, that they agree on where this forest is located, and that it is important to maintain and protect it. In other words, they substantially agree on a significant *what*. If they are able to consciously embrace this broader agreement, new ways to navigate their specific differences may emerge.

2. A slightly more mundane, and perhaps more familiar scenario involves two adults who love each other and share a living space, but who do not share the same relationship with air temperature. As long as they focus on their different comfort levels with various thermostat settings, they remain stuck in a pattern in which one is comfortable while the other is not, or they compromise so they are both regularly, albeit only slightly, uncomfortable. If they can step back and find a "mutual *what we want*" – something like *we want both of us to be comfortable with the temperature in our home*, more possibilities emerge. With a common goal rather than annoying differences as their starting point, everything from layered clothing, additional heating zone(s), portable heaters, fans, etc. comes into play, perhaps with some resent-free seasonal compromise as well.

3. Despite models and examples from around the world, the principals in the Insurance-Pharmaceutical-Medical-Industrial-Government Complex[2] do not or cannot agree on whether all citizens of the United States should have access to affordable, competent health care. Most seem to disagree on this larger *what,* and those who do agree on the *what* seem unable to agree on the *how.*

Chapter Five briefly introduced the concept of *orienting generalizations,*[3] which, simply put, refers to stepping back from an issue far enough in order find a level at which opponents can agree (*oh yes, we're definitely talking about the same forest...or being comfortable in our home*). Consider this rather striking contrast from Salvador Sanabria, a former Salvadoran guerilla and law student, when he served as part of a reconciliation team visiting Bosnia in 1997:

> "These people don't want peace. They want revenge. After 12 years of war in my country, we realized that no one could win. Both sides were exhausted, so we settled for peace. These people have not reached that point.

They still have two or three more years of killing in them." [4]

Sanabria spoke from the perspective of a war veteran who, along with his enemy, had recognized a shared desire for peace amid a shared exhaustion despite opposing reasons and desires to "win." He further recognized that the Croats, Muslims and Serbs with whom his team met were not yet able to step back far enough and find such a common goal – a similarity or orienting generalization that would allow them to stop killing each other.

Fortunately, most of our disagreements do not match the scope, scale and slaughter that accompany civil war. Still, we dig in, arm ourselves with the arguments of our beliefs, and label, generalize and insult our perceived 'enemy' as they do us.

On a more 'ordinary,' practical level, each of us who is interested in conversations that minimize or eliminate differences rather than maximizing or creating them might begin to look for the relevant, respective *what's* and *how's* that inform our disagreements, share what we see with our perceived opponent(s), and in the best of circumstances, even agree to step back *together* until our views are broad and/or deep enough that we find a shared perspective – an orienting generalization. Definitely noble work, not easy, and inevitably worthwhile – perhaps invaluable.

Two final points:

- The process of engaging conversation that recognizes similarities and is grounded in genuine curiosity and a desire to learn and understand, as discussed in Chapter Eight, is easier when both (or all) parties recognize and embrace such recognition and grounding.

- In the absence of such mutuality, it falls upon the courage, strength and vulnerability of those who do embrace this level of engagement to proceed in difficult conversations in ways that honor their embrace without putting themselves or others in serious danger – whether, physical, emotional or any other meaning of that word. Said differently, those who see more of the picture, see it more clearly, and both seek and can hold more perspectives, have more responsibility in a given conversation.

## The Trees Are Blocking My View of the Forest

One way to begin recognizing and pointing out similarities in difficult conversations:

- Begin by looking for similarities in situations in which the stakes are low – where the danger is slight and more of an inconvenience than anything else. Where, even if the "other" relentlessly holds his or her position and a worst-case scenario ensues, you will be all right. Having found a "low-stake" situation, invite the other to consider the similarity you've identified. "The story I'm telling myself..." on pp. 54-55 might be a useful way into this.

    o While perhaps an oversimplified example, a healthy, loving parent's or teacher's interactions with a young child, with very rare exceptions, are characterized by the adult's seeing more of what's going on, seeing more clearly, being capable of holding more perspectives than the child, and therefore having more responsibility in the interaction.

    o The terrain surrounding difficult interactions among adults is a bit more uncertain. Who's to say who sees more or more clearly, or holds more perspectives? A thorough exploration of those questions is beyond this book's scope. For now, a genuine embrace of Chapter Eight's focus on engaging conversation in order to learn, clarify and understand can go a long way toward seeing more and seeing more clearly.

In Chapter Ten we'll explore the value of agreeing to, and actually staying focused on, the specific content of the current conversation.

---

[1] We're using "generic, general and fictional" examples in order to make the point, and not pretend to resolve a real-world issue in a single paragraph in a book about communication.

[2] This language, in lieu of "healthcare system" is a bit hyperbolic, albeit accurate, in my view. It is in some ways antithetical to the theme of this book. Please forgive me.

[3] Wilber, Ken. *Sex, Ecology, Spirituality: The Spirit of Evolution.* Boston: Shambhala, 1995 (xiii-ix).

[4] Ryback, Timothy W. "Violence Therapy for a Country in Denial." *New York Times Magazine.* 30 November 1997, sec. 6: 120-23. Archive: https://www.nytimes.com/1997/11/30/magazine/violence-therapy-for-a-country-in-denial.html

# 10.

## Committing to and Actually Staying Focused on the Topic of the Current Conversation

Alert: this chapter's focus on staying focused raises more questions than it answers and points to additional reading that informs the topic.

Think about any common family or workplace disagreement where the initial statement addresses some specific transgression (real or imagined) like clothes not put away, lights left on, staying out later than expected without calling or texting, arriving to work late, not getting a task done on time, etc. Often, when the accused responds to the accusation, what follows may include the accused's pointing out some flaw or transgression of the accuser, and/or the accuser's expanding the initial, specific complaint about the accused to an overall criticism of who and how he or she is (while I've never experienced any of this personally, I've heard a lot about it from the less fortunate). Several ongoing examples follow.

Many arguments about abortion are characterized by people's positions on several related, but separate issues: a woman's right to make her own choices about her body; a human fetus's right to life; and *law* as handed down and/or interpreted by various religions, governments and science, among others. Rarely, if ever, is *one* of these the single focus of a conversation.[1]

Arguments in favor of and in opposition to proposed gun legislation intended to reduce the number of gun-related deaths in the United States include disagreements on how to interpret the second amendment to the country's Constitution; whether or not it's guns or people (or both) responsible for these gunshot deaths; contrasting U.S. laws and culture with those of other countries that have significantly fewer gunshot deaths; and how gun manufacturers' profits are used to lobby and support lawmakers' political campaigns, among others.

Listen to or read the rhetoric around the accessibility-to-affordable healthcare debate in the U.S. (yes, *that* again). Among the directions that conversation might go are whether healthcare is a right or a privilege; why the alleged wealthiest country in the world does not provide its citizens with the same level of healthcare as most other post-industrial countries; why the insurance industry wields more power than healthcare professionals when it comes to what services can be provided and under what conditions; why pharmaceutical companies produce billions of profit dollars while many drugs remain unaffordable to those who would benefit from them. There are, as you know, more directions this conversation might go.

Finally, if you have the stomach for it, read or listen to virtually any political debate or press conference. Rarely are the questions asked actually answered (an interesting exception to this is some state and local leaders during the COVID-19 pandemic; e.g. New York's Governor Andrew Cuomo[2]); often the moderators or journalists are engaged in proving a point rather than genuine journalistic inquiry intended to inform the public for the greater good; most of the politicians give short shrift to what they hope to avoid and 'much longer shrift' to the sound bites and slogans that their handlers believe are most expedient.

What's someone who deeply wants to engage authentic dialogue on one thing at a time to do?

The answers to this are complex and manifold. Culture (beliefs, worldviews, values), society (systems, infrastructure and environment) and individual intention (whether conscious or not) play major roles in making it more difficult for us to focus, and in discouraging us from focusing, on a single issue in conversation. Whether we're speaking about in-person disagreements, social media slugfests, televised or streamed eye-rolling contests among 'experts,' or any other conversational exchange, the combined effects of limited time, limited attention span, complex issues, dissimilar knowledge, ignorance,[3] training, experience, awareness, purpose, etc. among participants, the *relative* 'safety and anonymity' of social media and the pressure to perform in public and perhaps win (or not lose) something, are not conducive to engaging in conversation in order to learn, understand and clarify.

One approach to beginning to address these issues is 'simply' to agree on some ground rules regarding the focus of a given conversation – what is within and outside the context of this particular exchange. This is not easy to do – especially on social media or within the confines of televised timeslots bounded by advertisers' appeals, and in light of any of the above mentioned dissimilarities among participants. Still, it is doable for folks who, indeed, have a shared purpose in their disagreement.

For more reading on this topic, see Jesse Singal's "The New Science of How to Argue—Constructively," and one of his sources, John Nerst, who coined the word *erisology* to capture the study of unsuccessful disagreement. Full links below.

> "You left the lights on again."
> "Is it supposed to rain tomorrow?"

Two ways you can explore the importance of staying on a topic:
1. Visit the online news source of your choice (online so you'll have immediate access to readers' comments on what you

read). Select and read an article or opinion piece that is of interest to you and that allows readers' comments. Get a sense of what you believe the piece focuses on and the extent to which you agree and/or disagree with the writer's views. Read as many comments as you have time to read with the intention of observing:

   a. The relevance of each comment to the initial piece – i.e. is the reader responding to the piece or using the comment to state his or her general view of things?

   b. Each commenter's use of and (in)ability to differentiate fact, opinion, generalizations, labels and insults.

   c. How your own biases, including cultural givens, may be at play as you read and observe.

2. The next time you and a friend, colleague or loved one have to work through a difference, suggest getting clear on what's in play and what's not for the content of the conversation. With the right person this can become a useful (and even fun) learning experience as you explore the boundaries of what's relevant and what's not.

~

In Chapter Eleven we'll explore the usefulness of listening for and feeling into the emotion behind your own and others' words.

---

[1]Each of these issues has merit and interrelates with the others. Our point here is to address them one at a time, and to avoid responding to a question about one of them with an opinion about another. Genuinely seeking an orienting generalization, while it may not *resolve* the disagreement, might help civilize the discussion.

[2]Citing Governor Cuomo here specifically refers to his daily interactions with the media during the pandemic, which is ongoing as this book goes to print. Lots of folks in and outside of New York have opinions about him and his work prior to the virus's devastating impact on his state, and

prior to his becoming governor. Those opinions are not relevant to the specific topic being discussed here (note the chapter title).

[3]*ignorance* in the denotative, not deprecatory, meaning of the word – not knowing something. We often throw words around (and at each other) without agreeing on what they mean. This includes, but is not limited to, the sweeping generalizations, labels and insults referred to in Chapters Four and Six.

**Resources**

Jesse Singal:
https://www.theatlantic.com/ideas/archive/2019/04/erisology-the-science-of-arguing-about-everything/586534/

John Nerst: https://everythingstudies.com/about/

John Nerst: https://everythingstudies.com/2016/01/12/erisology/

# Part Five

*Emotion, Empathy and Ripple Effects
– Feeling, Honoring and
Regulating Emotions*

# 11.

# Listening for and Feeling into the Emotions that Lead to and Emerge from Your Own and Others' Words and Actions

**Note:** Information regarding emotional intelligence or competence is abundant. Different definitions and models make it clear that the scientific (research-based) definitions are often different from definitions that are popular in the media. In this chapter, emotional intelligence refers to *the ability to understand and manage emotional encounters – an ability that includes noticing, understanding and regulating emotions in oneself, noticing and understanding emotions in others, and directing emotions toward constructive behavior.*[1]

This chapter explores the value of understanding emotional encounters in conversation, and does not attempt to "teach" emotional intelligence. Toward that end, one very simple and extremely useful (in the best meaning of that word) models of how our emotions emerge from the stories we tell and our interpretations of events and language appears in *Crucial Conversations,* where the authors depict a "Path to Action"[2] in which something happens, we very quickly tell ourselves a story about or interpret it, we experience an emotion based on our story/interpretation, and then we act or speak based on the emotion that's based on our story, and not on what actually happened. Learning to recognize and interrupt this "path" is an essential step toward understanding, managing and regulating our emotions.

A slightly different version of this process is the late Chris Argyris's "Ladder of Inference,"[3] which zeroes in on the impact of what we do with our stories or interpretations. Argyris offers us a "reflexive loop," in which we first *select data* from what we observe, then *add our personal and cultural meaning* (givens), followed by *assumptions* based on the meaning we add, from which we then *draw conclusions* and *adopt beliefs* – which will impact what data we select the next time we observe something or something happens.

Both the Path to Action and the Ladder of Inference make it clear that our emotions are often, if not always, based on *our own responses to, stories about* and *interpretations of* what happens in the world – what someone else does or says, and rarely on the actual, external doing or saying. Here's an example. Less than 48 hours before the first draft of this chapter was finished, Tiger Woods won the 2019 Masters tournament (a factual, external event). Thomas Friedman's *New York Times* column (based on his own observations, selected data, assumptions, conclusions and beliefs) about the win led to over 600 comments from readers who responded according to their own interpretations/reflexive loops.[4]

We continue here as if you are willing to read the column and some of the comments. First, 'listen' for and feel into the emotions behind Friedman's piece *and* his readers' comments – some of whom respond to the column, some to the win, some to their general sense of Tiger Woods, and some to some combination thereof. What selected data, added meaning, and consequent assumptions, conclusions and beliefs are operating behind these diverse *amazed, compassionate, angry, resentful, frustrated, proud, disgusted, inspired, irritated, thrilled, grateful, discouraged, apathetic,* etc. responses? Second, we can apply that same listening for and feeling into *our own emotional responses* to what we read (and how we feel about the win).

While any one of us can begin to explore the above question for a given commenter, our ability to respond with some basic level of accuracy and competence is tied to our awareness of and ability to name, understand and regulate our own emotions. The Yale Center for Emotional Intelligence[5] has developed a research-based RULER program that helps participants **R**ecognize, **U**nderstand, **L**abel, **E**xpress and **R**egulate emotions. The process includes rating from 1-10 how one feels in a given moment on two scales – from low to high intensity/energy, and from unpleasant to pleasant. The rating leads to one of 100 emotion labels[6] for how we feel – providing an opportunity to build our emotional vocabulary in the process. The center has developed an online app[7] as well.

As we begin to bring this chapter to a close, we'll take a brief, stereotypical, and by no means definitive, look at an example[8] of anger. Why anger? Familiarity. In virtually every introductory poetry-writing workshop I've offered – to 3rd-graders, seniors and everyone in-between, virtually everyone finds it relatively easy to write images of anger or fear.

1. Two parents are talking while keeping an eye on their two young children who are playing with a ball. When the ball bounces toward the street, one child chases it, a parent runs after the child, and a car comes to a screeching halt as the parent aggressively pulls the child out of harm's way.
    a. The parent immediately yells at the child, repeating various warnings about the street, looking both ways, etc. The apparent emotion is anger.
    b. Beneath the anger is caring – if the parent didn't care about the child, anger would not have emerged. Between the caring and the anger, often, is fear: the parent cares; the child is in danger, so fear arises; the child is now safe, so the caring and fear manifest as anger directed at the child. What happens *next* is contingent upon the parent's

emotional competence. Once the immediate moment of warnings and yelling passes, still holding the child with some powerful physical energy:

    i. the parent might choose a violent response, hit the child, and continue yelling.
    ii. the parent might see the child's own fear, bring him or her close in a compassionate hug, and begin to comfort the child (and him- or herself as well in so doing).
    iii. the parent might ____ (fill in your own).

Whether we use this example, that of two drivers immediately after a fender-bender, divorce negotiations, child custody proceedings, strongly held religious or political positions, or any scenario in which strong emotion arises, the extent to which the individuals involved can recognize, understand and regulate their emotions, along with their cultural and personal givens, personality tendencies and other habits of mind will play a significant role in how the process unfolds.

In conclusion, emotions can run high in robust conversation – especially, but not only, when characterized by disagreement. Our ability to recognize, comprehend, name and regulate our own emotions can help deepen our understanding of what happens to us in highly charged encounters, and is an essential step if we want to understand others' emotional responses.

## What You Did Made Me Angry

Two ways to begin to explore emotions:

1. The next time you notice a strong emotion, pleasant or unpleasant, pause and explore what might be behind it; more specifically, what's the story you're telling yourself about some person, event or issue, that's bringing this emotion up. Once you're able to find the story, explore what

information the emotion has for you. What can you learn about yourself from this emotion?

2. Work with your emotional vocabulary and competence. The links provided at the end of the chapter provide places to start. There is (perhaps too) much more available online for your reading, listening and experiencing pleasure.

One caveat: explore your own stories and emotions first; avoid pointing out others' – especially if you love them.

~

In Chapter Twelve we'll explore the possibility and process of understanding, feeling, embodying and telling another's story as if it were our own.

---

[1]Paraphrase from *Emotional Intelligence: A Coaching Masterclass* (online): https://positivepsychology.com/course/a-coaching-masterclass-on-emotional-intelligence/

[2]Patterson, Kerry, and Joseph Grenny, et al. *Crucial Conversations: Tools for Talking When the Stakes Are High.* New York: McGraw-Hill, 2002, pp. 93-118.

[3]Abundant links to images and writing about the Ladder of Inference and Path to Action are available online. The following link provides images of both on a single page:
https://reggiemarra.files.wordpress.com/2019/04/ladder-of-inf-and-path-to-action.pdf

[4]Working with this column and the comments involves a process similar to the exercise in Chapter Ten, pp. 67-68, but with a different intention. There we were looking for facts, opinions and generalizations in relationship to a focus on one topic; here, we're curious about what informs a given writer's view.
https://www.nytimes.com/2019/04/15/opinion/tiger-woods-masters.html?action=click&module=Opinion&pgtype=Homepage

[5] Yale Center for Emotional Intelligence/RULER: https://www.rulerapproach.org/solutions/

[6] The Emotion Meter (Yale Center for Emotional Intelligence): https://reggiemarra.files.wordpress.com/2019/04/emo-meter.pdf

[7] Mood Meter App through the Yale Center for Emotional Intelligence: http://ei.yale.edu/mood-meter-app/

[8] For a more detailed look at a similar example, among others, in the context of one western approach to Zen Buddhism in the 21st Century, see *The Heart of Zen* by Junpo Denis Kelly and Keith Martin-Smith. Full reference in Selected Resources.

## 12.

## Understanding, Feeling, Embodying and Telling Another's Story as if It Were Your Own

Most of us, during our 'single-digit years', hear a parent or teacher talking about the importance of never criticizing someone until we've walked a mile in his or her shoes. My first exposure to this directed me to *never criticize another warrior until I had walked a mile in his moccasins.* The message was and still is clear and valuable, and my adolescent self eventually saw it as another iteration of not judging my neighbor – of getting the plank out of my own eye before I pointed out the speck in someone else's, of seeing someone else, another warrior or my neighbor, in the context of his or her own life and history, and not just through my own.

There is, however, as I'm sure you know (gentle reader), a big difference between eventually being able *to see* something and authentically embodying and living it. In my direct experience of sincerely trying to walk a mile in someone's shoes – of understanding him or her amid his or her unique circumstances, and in my observing others attempting this same task, it is clear that a significant majority of us who attempt this often succeed reasonably well in fitting into the shoes and walking the mile, but we do so *as ourselves* and not as the other. More concretely, and somewhat simplistically, to make the point:

> Our neighbor is navigating some troubling behavior with his 16-year-old. We feel judgment arise because we imagine we might navigate it differently, but then diligently remember the old moccasin-mile lesson from childhood and attempt to put ourselves into the details of our neighbor's and his kid's circumstances in order to better understand – and perhaps provide support. More often than not *that's exactly what we do*. We put *ourselves* into *their* circumstances, but we have no idea what those circumstances look and feel like through *their* cultural givens, history and view of the world. What we need to do is find a way to feel and see things as our neighbor does *while he's wearing his shoes*, and not just feel and see things *as we do* when we try them on.

We are taught to look at things and people and to try to understand them, and if we're sincere in our looking and trying, we can understand some things and people in increasingly deeper ways – and that's great. What we're talking about here, however, is celebrating and building on this *looking at* people and learning to *look as* them – to see as they see, feel as they feel, in order to better understand what it's like to *be them* in *their* circumstances (again, rather than be *ourselves* in their circumstances). No small task. So, while it's helpful to try to feel the impact of the rebellious adolescent, divorce, diagnosis, pink slip, lottery win, lack of basic healthcare, sense of being inadequate or unloved, etc., it's more helpful if we can do so with an embodiment of *the other's sense and way of being* in and moving through the world.

Laura Divine writes that this *looking as* another "involves being able to look through their eyes, from their body-mind-soul in order to get a sense of their unique way of seeing and relating…. This process of Looking AS is a powerful practice of embodied perspective taking."[1] It's not something we can simply decide to do; *it requires that we first become competent in looking both at and as ourselves* – recognizing and embodying what it feels like to be who *we* are with our history, personality, biases and overall worldview, a competence that allows us to better differentiate what is ours and what is someone else's.[2]

Now, when we see our neighbor struggling with his kid, we can differentiate the influence of *our own* experience of adolescence and parenthood from our neighbor's particular history and experience, and better see and feel the current issue through *his* eyes and body, and perhaps revise our navigational advice (or keep it to ourselves). Making this move does not prevent us from sharing the benefit of our own story and learning, from which our neighbor might actually benefit at an appropriate time and place. Rather, again, it 'simply' allows us to differentiate what is ours and what is his or hers, and to honor both – an honoring that comes in handy the next time the roles are reversed, when our neighbor offers to help us through some difficulty.

As we become increasingly competent looking first *at* and *as* ourselves, and then looking *at* and *as* others, what we and others say and do *begins to make increasingly more sense* – even if we believe it would be best to revise (or end) our or their sayings and doings. When we take the time to listen, look, recognize, understand and attempt to embody, we can put ourselves into their story and tell it as though it were our own.[3]

Imagine being able to do this amid a conversation in which you and another disagree.

## Try This Story on for Size

One way to begin to explore is to convene with a friend, family member or colleague with whom you have a longstanding and trusting relationship. Select a topic that is of interest to you both, whether you are in agreement or not, and take turns listening to each other, asking each other questions, and getting as clear as you can on each other's position and reasoning. Then take turns speaking as though you are each other. This mostly risk-free exercise allows you to begin to build the muscles required to tell another's story as if it were your own.

~

Chapter Thirteen explores the question, "Who stands to lose, and how and what will they lose, and who stands to win, and how and what will they win, if what I promote truly manifests and what I protest truly disappears?"

---

[1] Divine, Laura. "Looking AT and Looking AS the Client: The Quadrants as a Type Structure Lens" *Journal of Integral Theory and Practice*, 4.1 (Spring 2009): 21-40. For more information: http://www.metaintegralstore.com/spring-2009-vol-4-no-1/looking-at-and-looking-as-the-client-the-quadrant-as-a-type-structure-lens. Laura Divine is a co-founder of Integral Coaching Canada. I completed their coach training program in 2011 and currently (2015-present) work with some of their students.

[2] See Chapters One, Two and Three to review personal history, personality, worldview and who (we think) we are.

[3] Some meeting or workshop "icebreaker" exercises skim the surface of this experience: a new acquaintance and I briefly share who we are with each other, and then introduce each other to the larger group – each of us speaking in first-person, as though we *are* the person we're introducing. For a much deeper dive into telling another's story as if it were our own, see the work of *Narrative 4,* an organization that uses "story exchange" to help young (and old) people develop empathy. "Narrative 4 harnesses the power of the story exchange to equip and embolden young adults to improve their lives, their communities, and the world." https://narrative4.com/

# 13.

## What's the Impact of (Not) Getting My Way: What Will Be Won and Lost, and by Whom?[1]

One of the "easiest" scenarios within which to explore these questions is in athletic competition. *Easiest* is in quotation marks because while participation in most sports does not typically carry with it the life-and-death ramifications of illness, injury, violent crime and war, it is neither necessarily *easy,* nor without its larger ramifications.[2] Simply put, when I win – when I get my way, my opponents lose, or at best, finish second. Healthy competitors accept and expect this, and – especially for those who learn from their wins and losses, begin to develop those physical, emotional, mental and spiritual "muscles" that allow them to "win with class" and "lose with dignity".

Whether we're exploring a child's earliest experiences with competition and final scores or an elite athlete's efforts to compete on a national or international stage, perspectives on winning and losing and the respective "muscles" these outcomes can build play an important role in the development of balance, resilience, compassion and empathy, among others.

Beyond athletics, these muscles will come in handy as we attempt to "win" – to get our way at work, in intimate relationship, as parents, as children, in the classroom, in court, on the playground, in the legislature, in the operating room, with the therapist, in the voting booth, on the street, in combat, on our death bed, and anywhere else we believe something important is at stake.

Consider these selected historical wins and losses, and then add others that are of particular interest to you:

- 1600 – Giordano Bruno is burned at the stake at the order of Pope Clement VIII for arguing first that the universe is spatially infinite (he asked if it's bounded, what's on the other side) and second that God is both transcendent and immanent.
- 1776 – British immigrants in North America declare their independence from British rule.
- 1863 – The Emancipation Proclamation declares all slaves in the United States free.
- 1865 – The 13th Amendment to the U.S. Constitution abolishes slavery, and the Ku Klux Klan is founded in Pulaski, Tennessee.
- 1870 – The 15th Amendment removes race, color and previous-condition-of-servitude restrictions from a man's right to vote.
- 1920 – The 19th Amendment removes gender restrictions so women can vote.
- 1924-1929 – Edwin Hubble, and later the telescope that bears his name, confirm Bruno's first point (above).
- 1945 – The first atomic bomb is detonated in New Mexico; then two are detonated by the United States over Japan.
- 1954 – Racial segregation in public schools in the United States is declared unconstitutional in *Brown v. Board of Education of Topeka.*

For each of these (and for other historical and current, public and personal events of your choosing) consider who won and who lost in the short term, who won and lost in the long term, what the winners and losers actually won and lost in each case, and who might still be winning and losing. Your worldview, which we explored in Chapters One, Two and Three, will influence how you respond to each of these – as my worldview influenced which examples to enlist (and the decision to write this book at all).

One of the most powerful change agents that produces winners and losers is technology – in the broadest meaning of that word. Who were and are the winners and losers with the emergence of intentional fire, the wheel, the firearm, pharmaceuticals, electricity, the internal combustion engine, the printing press, the assembly line, human flight, the computer and robotics, among many others? Again, check in with the worldview behind your responses as you explore this question.

So *"what do these selected explorations of sports, history and technology have to do with who wins and loses when I do or do not get my way in conversation?"* you might ask? Concretely and specifically, not very much; conceptually and generally, everything. In Chapter Seven we explored our human tendency to ascribe meaning or make interpretations before we truly know what something *means* – what might be an accurate interpretation of an event. We spoke about getting comfortable with *not knowing* on the path of learning.

With every stance we take, every stand we make, every debate we engage – whether about which movie to watch, where to buy the groceries, going back to school, dealing with a bully, helping our kid navigate a first heartbreak, whom to support in an election, having the surgery, going to war, etc., etc., etc. – we are choosing to support a position that will lead to winners and losers, often in very minor and often in very major ways. At our best it makes sense to know, or at least investigate, who these winners and losers may be and what and how much they stand to win or lose, so we have a sense of the not-so-obvious, prospective impact of what we argue for and against. At the risk of stating the obvious, our ability to look as others, to be able to tell others' stories as if they were our own, is an essential skill if we are to authentically and competently investigate the ramifications of getting or not getting what we argue for.

Perhaps the most often cited and rarely lived example of this in contemporary Western culture is the Iroquois Confederacy's philosophy that each of us should take into account the impact our decisions will have seven generations into the future.[3]

> Oh. I Hadn't Thought of That.

Two ways to begin to explore these prospective impacts of our positions in conversation:

1. Select one or more of the historical events on page 84, or use another event of particular interest to you, and explore the short and long term impacts of the event: who "won," who "lost" and what and how much did they win and lose.

2. Pick a current position you hold on an issue that is important to you. Imagine what would happen if you got your way, and if you did not get your way. In either case, who wins, who loses, and what and how much do they win and lose?

~

In Chapter Fourteen we'll take a look at the difference between "truth" and "truthfulness" and explore why each is important.

---

[1]This chapter title emerged through seeds planted by Neil Postman's six questions (among others) around solving problems through change and technology: 1) What's the problem? 2) Whose problem is it? 3) What new problems will be created by solving an old one? 4) What people and institutions will be most seriously harmed? 5) What changes in language are occurring? 6) What new sources of economic and political power will emerge? From "Staying Sane in a Technological Society: Six Questions in Search of an Answer." *Lapis.* 7 (1998): 53-57.

[2] For a more in-depth exploration of the ramifications of participating, competing, and winning and losing in youth, interscholastic and some intercollegiate sport, see *The Quality of Effort: Integrity in Sport and Life for Student-Athletes, Parents and Coaches*. 2nd edition (2013). The book acknowledges, but does not focus on those professional and intercollegiate competitions in which billions of media, advertising, sponsorship, corporate and organizational dollars are in play and at stake – where much winning and losing goes on beyond what we see among the competitors in practice and in the arena.

[3] Many indigenous peoples on the planet embrace this philosophy, and a significant number of organizations, both for- and not-for-profit make use of "seventh generation" language.

Part Six

*Understanding "Truth" and Truthfulness"*

# 14.

## The Truth, the Whole Truth and Nothing but the Truth[1]

While the importance of a commitment to truth is implicit in our exploration of opinion and fact in Chapter Five (and, I hope, throughout this book and the rest of our lives), truth deserves a more explicit role in this book. Most of us have experienced, heard or read somewhere along the line that prior to testifying in court, we promise, swear or affirm that we will tell the truth, the whole truth and nothing but the truth. Those words are generally familiar and carry meaning that is, or seems to be, obvious (which won't stop me from reviewing them):

- Tell **the truth:** answer the question that was asked or address the topic at hand and don't lie.
- Tell the **whole truth:** don't omit anything regarding your answer to the question or your knowledge of the topic.
- Tell **nothing but the truth:** don't add or intermingle anything that's not true in order to help your cause.

While this chapter and book are not explicitly concerned with what happens under oath in a court of law, these three tenets are worth keeping in mind as we navigate the fate of truth in our day-to-day conversations – whether we are disagreeing, agreeing or casually passing the time. Also worth keeping in mind is the distinction between "the truth" and "truthfulness" – a distinction that informs this chapter, and that I believe is accurate and useful. As we'll use these terms here:

- **the truth** refers to what is empirically provable[2] and can be agreed upon by honest, competent observers who have no interest or investment in the truth being one way or another;
- **truthfulness** refers to an individual's honesty – choosing in any given moment to be honest – "tell the truth" as he or she understands it; it is possible to be truthful and neither know nor tell what is empirically true.

If we revisit Chapter Five's auto collision at the four-way stop sign, the truth is that two cars made contact and sustained damage. Assuming for a moment that the drivers are honest and do not want to wrongfully vilify each other, each of them might be *truthful* in explaining what they *think* caused the accident (beyond agreeing that the cars collided and sustained damage), and each may be completely accurate, completely off the mark or somewhat accurate and somewhat off the mark amid their truthfulness.[3]

That's a simple example and enough to make the point. In our disagreements and agreements with others, underlying our commitment to differentiating fact and opinion must be a corresponding understanding of and commitment to *the* truth and *our* truthfulness. Clarity of language is essential for such a commitment, as is a willingness to do the work that clarification requires.

The complexities that characterize the content of much contemporary disagreement, the over-abundance of easily accessible information and much intentional misinformation that internet sources invite and allow, and selectively edited and sound-bitten televised news offerings render "the truth" at best difficult to identify, and at worst an unwelcome and troublesome nuisance, especially for those who tend to benefit from keeping certain "whole truths" hidden. The ramifications of this complex overabundance are especially evident among individuals who are more committed to incessantly reasserting their biases in order to "win" the social media tit-for-tat or televised eye-rolling-and-shouting match of the day than to working toward an agreed-upon "truth" and negotiating in good faith with others who differ regarding how to interpret and act on this truth – whether it concerns local, national or international policy, buying or leasing a vehicle, which movie to see, which diet to try or which get-rich-quick scheme to purchase (or sell).

We return to intention. Why are you, am I, are we, in this conversation at all, and what, if anything, does the truth, or our respective 'truthfulnesses' have to do with it? If nothing, then why bother? If something, why not everything? If everything, how might each of us *behave* if we were genuinely concerned with and committed to the truth and to being increasingly able to see each other's truthfulness even as we disagree?

Don't look to apparent or titular leaders as exemplars for this behavior. Very few of them are up for the challenge, and while some may be, your best bet is to look within. Be the conversationalist you aspire to be. Take the risk of showing up with the intentions of understanding and learning, with nothing to prove, nothing to defend and nothing to lose.

> ### *De Veritate Disputandum Est*[4]

One way, among many, to explore the relationship between truth and truthfulness:

1. Think back to a recent disagreement you had with someone about whom you care deeply.

    a. Honestly ask yourself if there's an empirical truth involved in the disagreement. If there is, identify it; if there's not, then you're working 'only' with opinions and truthfulness.

    b. Either way, fearlessly explore how truthful you were in the disagreement: to what extent did you state your opinion as fact, try to win at any cost or ignore (fail to attempt to look *as*, or even try on the shoes of) this person you care about?

c. If you find yourself trying to explore the other person's truthfulness, rather than your own, through these steps, you're just looking for trouble. Don't do it.

~

In Chapter Fifteen we'll take a brief look at the preceding chapters and make some final comments before sending you on your way.

———

[1]What we're attempting to point to in this chapter (and in this book) are useful, practical considerations for authentic conversation. We're not delving into differentiating the mystical/spiritual realms of what is manifest-relative truth or Unmanifest-Absolute Truth; there is a time and place for these (even if time and place only exist on the manifest-relative plane) and this is neither.

[2]What is "empirically provable" – i.e. true, shifts over time and with development. Cultures have ever-evolving maps of "reality" that represent what they believe is true. If something fits the current map, it's "true,"; if it doesn't, it's not. E.g. over millennia it was true that first the earth (religion's view), then the sun (early science's view) was the center of the universe; the current (more advanced science) truth tells us that the universe is ever-expanding, and that neither our planet nor our sun is at the center. The technological innovations referred to in Chapter 13 each shifted "the truth" in many ways: intentional fire, the wheel, the printing press, the internal combustion engine, and the "computer" are just a few examples. Parker J. Palmer, in his *The Courage to Teach*, wonderfully captures empirical truth's shifting over time and with development: *"[T]ruth is an eternal conversation about things that matter, conducted with passion and discipline"* (p. 104). Italics in original.

[3]Distraction, confusion, mechanical failure, etc. may come into play here, and even if each driver is honest (i.e. truthful), when faced with the possibility of insurance premiums going up, moving violations, having to explain to parents or spouses what happened, the temptation not to tell

the whole truth or to in some way embellish it (telling something beyond the truth) might be tempting – putting them at odds with both "truthfulness" and the "truth." That the two cars collided is the truth, as far as it goes. If our goal were to get to the fictional truth of the fictional cause(s) of this fictional collision we'd pursue this further. It's not, so we won't. Why would we do that anyway? More important is our willingness and ability to explore our real-life examples of the themes (not the actual content) that this fictional fender-bender brings forth.

[4] "About matters of truth, dispute is fruitful." From Mortimer Adler's *Six Great Ideas,* p. 58. See Selected Resources.

# 15.

## Stepping Back and Moving Forward: Bringing a Bigger Picture into View

As a "handy reference" to accompany the brief conclusion below, here are the section and chapter titles we've explored together:

– Introduction

**Knowing Yourself, Your Biases and Your View – Working with What and How You See**

> 1 – Who (You Think) You Are in Conversation, Part 1 – The Culture Thing
>
> 2 – Who (You Think) You Are in Conversation, Part 2 – Within and Beyond Culture
>
> 3 – Recognizing and Suspending Preconceptions, Judgments and Assumptions

**Honoring Facts and Identifying Opinions – Really? Will That Hold Up in Court or in the Laboratory?**

> 4 – Avoiding Labels, Insults and Sweeping Generalizations
>
> 5 – Getting Clear on and Honoring the Difference Between Opinion and Fact

6 – Antidotes for Generalizations, Labels and Insults: Get Specific, Factual, Personal and Aware of Others

**Learning Intentionally – How Do You Want to Be, and What Do You Hope for, in this Conversation?**

7 – Curiosity, Knowing and Not Knowing on the Path of Learning

8 – Conversing in Order to Learn, Understand and Gain Clarity, Rather than Trying to Teach, Persuade or Disprove

**Acknowledging the Forest and Staying on the Path – Wow, *You're Human Too!***

9 – Finding Similarities as Well as Differences in Disagreement

10 – Committing to and Actually Staying Focused on the Topic of the Current Conversation

**Emotion, Empathy and Ripple Effects – Feeling, Honoring and Regulating Emotions**

11 – Listening for and Feeling into the Emotions that Lead to and Emerge from Your Own and Others' Words and Actions

12 – Understanding, Feeling, Embodying and Telling Another's Story as if It Were Your Own

13 – What's the Impact of (Not) Getting My Way: What Will Be Won and Lost and by Whom?

**Understanding "Truth" and "Truthfulness"**

14 – The Truth, the Whole Truth and Nothing but the Truth

While the content of some of these chapters is more complex, and requires more work than others, each provides a foundational element for conversation that does more good than harm.[1] Some are more or less "mechanical" skills that can be learned, but even those will be interpreted, understood and manifested differently based on the conversationalists' respective worldviews (Chapters One, Two and Three), and the extent to which they are aware of their worldviews (i.e. do they have a worldview or does a worldview have them?). The worldview will also impact the intentional choices that are available to (that can be seen and acted on by) each of us and our partners in conversation.

Generally, someone who primarily identifies with and operates through a fundamentalist, absolutist, closed, black-and-white view of the world, whether conservative or liberal,[2] is more likely to intend to teach or persuade, as opposed to learn and understand, in conversation, than is someone who primarily identifies with a more "scientific," rational, evidence-based, okay-with-the-gray view of the world, and who is more open to curiosity, following the evidence, understanding and clarifying. In the most extreme cases of these two views (closed or open), the individuals effectively speak different languages – as much a barrier to resolving a dispute as, and perhaps more than, any of the content about which they disagree.

Each of us needs to ask how important consciously civil and intentionally mutually beneficial and respectful conversation is to us. Several chapters of this book request a somewhat deep dive in order to be understood and embodied. Any one of them can enhance the quality of conversation. If you choose to begin, perhaps begin with something that feels easier; or begin with the one you know you need to develop; or take them in chapter order.

The essence of this book goes beyond, and does not address what I consider the more conventional "basic skills" of conversation such as: *don't multitask* (pay attention/be fully present); *use open-ended questions* (allow and invite reflection and thought by minimizing questions that can be answered with a *yes* or a *no*); *be brief* (know, and get to, your point). Each of these has value and is worth abiding, but even taken together, they provide an incomplete approach to conversation if we truly want to do more good than harm. Any one of these basic skills can be manipulated and used effectively by the local (or online) scammer or snake-oil salesperson.

Conversations that do more good than harm can be smoother with these basic skills, but they cannot take place without the intentional, authentic and essential inner work that deepens awareness of self, other, and context.

The world needs you. The world needs us. We need each other.

Just begin. Practice.

---

[1] Some wise folks (not wise guys, quite a few of whom I know and love) suggested that this subtitle, "Doing More Good than Harm in Conversation," sets a rather low bar – that we need more than that, and I agree. *Doing great things and no harm* is a loftier and preferred goal. In light of much of what I hear and read every day, however, this low bar, or incremental step, is exactly what we need right now.

[2] *Fundamentalist* and *absolutist* are descriptions at times mistakenly aligned with the *content,* or the "what" of a given belief system (e.g. "fundamentalist" Christianity or Islam typically refers to the extreme conservative, absolute or literal content of either religion) rather than the *manner* in which the belief system is held, or the "how" of the system. As these words are used here, they refer to the latter. We can (and do) pour conservatism, liberalism and other "isms" into extreme, absolutist, fundamentalist "containers" or worldviews.

# SELECTED RESOURCES

## Conversation-Specific

*Books* (Among *many*, here are two I've read and use, and one, forthcoming as this book goes to press, that I trust will match or exceed the value of the author's previous work).

Hamilton, Diane Musho. *Everything Is Workable: A Zen Approach to Conflict Resolution.* Boston: Shambhala, 2013.

Hamilton, Diane Musho, Gabriel Menegale Wilson and Kimberly Loh. *Compassionate Conversations: How to Speak and Listen from the Heart.* Boston: Shambhala, 2020.

Patterson, Kerry, and Joseph Grenny, et al. *Crucial Conversations: Tools for Talking When the Stakes Are High.* New York: McGraw-Hill, 2002.

*Online*

These sites provide various strategies and approaches to conversation. All are active and functional as we go to press.

How to Have a Conversation with Your Angry Uncle Over the Holidays: https://www.nytimes.com/interactive/2018/11/18/opinion/thanksgiving-family-argue-chat-bot.html?action=click&module=Opinion&pgtype=Homepage

Living Room Conversations: https://www.livingroomconversations.org/

On Being: Civil Conversations Project: https://onbeing.org/civil-conversations-project/

Institute for Social Renewal: http://socialrenewal.com/the-art-of-conscious-conversation/

## Politics

These two sites provide insight into how various media cover the news. They are also useful guides to help us recognize our own biases (i.e. which media and specific stories rile us up).

https://www.allsides.com/unbiased-balanced-news
Allsides rates media and story coverage from Left to Center to Right (L L C R R) making it easier to track who's covering what, and how various media cover and frame the same story.

https://www.axios.com
Axios believes there is "enough noise and our job is to sort through this," and that "truth and facts exist and must be highlighted, repeated, defended and cherished…"

---

*Chapter One*

Merton, Thomas. "The Inner Experience." *Thomas Merton: Spiritual Master.* Ed. Lawrence S. Cunningham. Mahwah NJ: Paulist, 1992, p. 295.

Wilber, Ken. *Integral Spirituality: A Startling New Role for Religion in the Modern and Postmodern World.* Boston: Integral-Shambhala, 2006, p. 277.

*Chapter Two*

The Enneagram:

https://www.enneagraminstitute.com/type-descriptions
https://www.enneagramworldwide.com/tour-the-nine-types/

Multiple Intelligences:

http://www.institute4learning.com/resources/

Integral Theory & Practice:

Wilber, Ken. *The Integral Vision: A Very Short Introduction to the Revolutionary Integral Approach to Life, God, the Universe, and Everything.* Boston: Shambhala, 2007.

Wilber, Ken, Terry Patten, et. al. *Integral Life Practice: A 21ˢᵗ-Century Blueprint for Physical Health, Emotional Balance, Mental Clarity, and*

*Spiritual Awakening.* Boston: Integral-Shambhala, 2008.

Culture, Illness and Trauma:

Maté, Gabor. *When the Body Says No: Exploring the Stress-Disease Connection.* Hoboken, NJ: Wiley & Sons, 2003.

Mehl-Medrona, Lewis. *Coyote Wisdom: The Power of Story in Healing.* Rochester, VT: Bear & Company, 2005.

Van der Kolk, Bessel. *The Body Keeps the Score: Brain, Mind and Body in the Healing of Trauma.* New York: Penguin, 2014.

Shadow:

Marra, Reggie. "Revisiting 'Donald Trump, Collective American Shadow, and the Better Angels of Our Nature.'" https://reggiemarra.com/2018/10/28/revisiting-donald-trump-collective-american-shadow-and-the-better-angels-of-our-nature/

Zweig, Connie, and Jeremiah Abrams, eds. *Meeting the Shadow: The Hidden Power of the Dark Side of Human Nature.* New York: Tarcher-Penguin, 1991.

*Chapter Three*

Kegan, Robert, and Lisa Laskow Lahey. *Immunity to Change: How to Overcome It and Unlock the Potential in Yourself and Your Organization.* Boston: Harvard Business, 2009. http://mindsatwork.com/

Katie, Byron. *Loving What Is: Four Questions That Can Change Your Life.* New York: Harmony, 2002. http://thework.com/en/do-work

*Chapter Four*

Lakoff, George, and Mark Johnson. *Metaphors We Live By.* Chicago: U of Chicago P, 1980, 2003.

*Chapter Five*

Wilber, Ken. *Sex, Ecology, Spirituality: The Spirit of Evolution.* Boston: Shambhala, 1995 (xiii-ix).

*Chapter Six* – n/a

*Chapter Seven*

    Master Seung Sahn:
https://tricycle.org/magazine/master-seung-sahn-1927-2004/

*Chapter Eight*

    Proprioceptive Writing:
http://pwriting.org/

    Council:

Zimmerman, Jack, in collaboration with Virginia Coyle. *The Way of Council.* Las Vegas: Bramble, 1996.

Animas Valley Institute: https://animas.org/

*Chapter Nine*

Ryback, Timothy W. "Violence Therapy for a Country in Denial." *New York Times Magazine.* 30 November 1997, sec. 6: 120-23. Archive: https://www.nytimes.com/1997/11/30/magazine/violence-therapy-for-a-country-in-denial.html

*Chapter Ten*

    Arguing Constructively:

Jesse Singal:
https://www.theatlantic.com/ideas/archive/2019/04/erisology-the-science-of-arguing-about-everything/586534/

John Nerst:
https://everythingstudies.com/about/
https://everythingstudies.com/2016/01/12/erisology/

*Chapter Eleven*

Emotions:

https://positivepsychology.com/course/a-coaching-masterclass-on-emotional-intelligence/

Patterson, Kerry, and Joseph Grenny, et al. *Crucial Conversations: Tools for Talking When the Stakes Are High.* New York: McGraw-Hill, 2002, pp. 93-118.

https://reggiemarra.files.wordpress.com/2019/04/ladder-of-inf-and-path-to-action.pdf

https://www.nytimes.com/2019/04/15/opinion/tiger-woods-masters.html?action=click&module=Opinion&pgtype=Homepage

https://www.rulerapproach.org/solutions/

https://reggiemarra.files.wordpress.com/2019/04/emo-meter.pdf

http://ei.yale.edu/mood-meter-app/

Kelly, Junpo Denis, and Keith Martin-Smith. *The Heart of Zen: Enlightenment, Emotional Maturity, and What It Really Takes for Spiritual Liberation.* Berkeley: North Atlantic, 2014.

*Chapter Twelve*

Looking AS:
Divine, Laura. "Looking AT and Looking AS the Client: The Quadrants as a Type Structure Lens" *Journal of Integral Theory and Practice*, 4.1 (Spring 2009): 21-40. http://www.metaintegralstore.com/spring-2009-vol-4-no-1/looking-at-and-looking-as-the-client-the-quadrant-as-a-type-structure-lens

Story Exchange:
https://narrative4.com/

~

*Chapter Thirteen*

    Winners and Losers:

Postman, Neil. "Staying Sane in a Technological Society: Six Questions in Search of an Answer." *Lapis.* 7 (1998): 53-57.

Marra, Reggie. *The Quality of Effort: Integrity in Sport and Life for Student-Athletes, Parents and Coaches.* 2nd ed. From the Heart, 2013.

*Chapter Fourteen*

    Truth:

Palmer, Parker J. *The Courage to Teach: Exploring the Inner Landscape of a Teacher's Life.* San Francisco: Jossey-Bass, 1998.

Adler, Mortimer. *Six Great Ideas.* New York: Macmillan, 1981.

*Chapter Fifteen* – n/a

REGGIE MARRA has conducted poetry-writing and adult development and healing workshops since 1997, including work with the NEA's Poetry Out Loud program, the National Association for Poetry Therapy, the Connecticut Higher Order Thinking (HOT) Schools program, the Transformative Language Arts Network, Teleosis Institute, the Arts Alliance of Northern New Hampshire, HealingNewtown, the National Speakers Association and in schools throughout the northeastern United States. Reggie is an Integral Master Coach,™ a Voice Dialogue practitioner through Bridgit Dengel Gaspard, and Nature Based Soulcraft® practitioner, through Bill Plotkin and Animas Valley Institute. Prior to 1997 he spent 21 years as a teacher, basketball coach and administrator in secondary and higher education.

https://reggiemarra.com/

In late 2019, with Kent Frazier, he co-founded the Fully Human at Work initiative:

https://fullyhumanatwork.com/

www.ingramcontent.com/pod-product-compliance
Lightning Source LLC
Chambersburg PA
CBHW022114090426

42743CB00008B/843